THE
Minneapolis Poet

Bruce Ario

Selected Poems 1980-2022

Edited by Dan Schneider

CONTENTS

The below essay follows the outlines concerning Fair Use of copyrighted works for critical and educational purposes, as outlined in the link and below:

https://www.copyright.gov/title17/92chap1.html#107

107. Limitations on exclusive rights: Fair use

Notwithstanding the provisions of sections 106 and 106A, the fair use of a copyrighted work, including such use by reproduction in copies or phonorecords or by any other means specified by that section, for purposes such as criticism, comment, news reporting, teaching (including multiple copies for classroom use), scholarship, or research, is not an infringement of copyright. In determining whether the use made of a work in any particular case is a fair use the factors to be considered shall include:

> (1) the purpose and character of the use, including whether such use is of a commercial nature or is for nonprofit educational purposes;

> (2) the nature of the copyrighted work;

> (3) the amount and substantiality of the portion used in relation to the copyrighted work as a whole; and

> (4) the effect of the use upon the potential market for or value of the copyrighted work.

The fact that a work is unpublished shall not itself bar a finding of fair use if such finding is made upon consideration of all the above factors.

Dan Schneider

Autumn, 2022

*****

Introducing Bruce Ario

The Man

Bruce Ario was a poet, and this essay will argue and prove that he was a great poet, for I am here to introduce Bruce Ario to the average poetry reader and into the pantheon of great poets.

Of course, like all things in life, he was also many other things: a writer of plays, novels, articles, essays, journals.... He was a friend, brother, son, employee, volunteer.... He was the survivor of a traumatic car accident and brain injury (TBI), mentally ill—and an exponent for that ill, an alcoholic, drug addict, sexual fetishist, and a formerly homeless person. He was a Born Again Christian, and a lifelong bachelor—not necessarily by choice—but most of all he was a poet: a *great* poet. Despite his varying senses of self, being a poet—and a Christian—were the two Twin Towers of Bruce's life.

In the rest of this essay I will refer to Bruce Ario simply as *Bruce*, as I and all about him knew him; not in the impersonal sense of *Ario*. Bruce lacked pretense and was personable to all he met, so referring to him by his first name seems correct and natural. Besides, as Bruce was the creator and master of the *ario* poetic form, which I shall show, and which will become manifest in this selection of his best poems, that word is far more cogent as a poetic form than a surname. Oh, I'm also the person that named the form after the man.

I knew Bruce for almost 30 years, having met him in 1993—either at a poetry reading at a long defunct cafe called the Coffee Gallery, at the southwestern corner of Franklin and Lyndale Avenues, in Minneapolis, or at a Saturday morning poetry group called Ophelia's Pale Lilies. I cannot recall which venue was the actual genesis of our artistic acquaintance and friendship, but it was one of those two. Bruce had been born and grown up in the city of Minneapolis, and its surrounds, and loved the city like he only also loved God and Bob Dylan. *St. Paul*? Eh.... Bruce was one of many Minneapolitans who rarely ventured to their city's twin. Of course, he did not drive, because of his accident, had no license, and bus schedules between the cities, even in the 1990s and early 2000s, were somewhat sketchy. In late 2003 I and my wife Jessica Schneider, after some personal and professional setbacks, moved from the Twin Cities area and down to Texas.

I had run the Uptown Poetry Group (UPG) for 8 years, at that point, meeting every 2nd and 3rd Friday of the month, and we ended it with 200 consecutive meetings in toto. Other than myself, who went to all 200 meetings, Bruce was the most steady UPGer, attending 180+ meetings. Overall, the UPG was unique amongst poetry groups, in the Twin Cities, or elsewhere, for we actually practiced good, fair criticism. If a poem was bad we openly stated so, explained why, and this sometimes led to people coming and going, because most arts critique groups are less about critique, and more about the participants needing an ego boost, or people just trying to use them as *de facto* singles groups. No poetry group I've ever been a part of elsewhere came close to the UPG's ability to produce great poetry, by individuals like me, Jess, Bruce, Don Moss, Art Durkee, Dave Nelson, Robert Newkirk, and a number of others. That's because I set the tone for both critical and poetic quality that defined the group as something different and better than other poetry groups. Many poets, including Bruce, hit their zenith in the art form while going to the UPG, and Bruce seemed to maintain that quality, and improve on it, in later poems. His pre-UPG corpus is far inferior to those poems written during the UPG's run (1995-2003) or even well after its end. In his last decade, it seems Bruce's poetic *batting average* increased, as quality work made up a larger percentage of his output. Not only that but all his post-UPG poems were better initially formed. The greats were still great but his lesser poems were also much better than earlier non-great poems. They had a higher floor of sound fundaments, if not ceiling; and this became evident not long after the bulk of this book was done, when I hired someone to look into Bruce's PC so I could uncover more of his verse. What I found will be contained in a second book of poems I will call *Final Poems*, and includes 198 more poems; including 9 more great arios. But few poets ever want to work hard enough to improve, especially if they have real talent. They often just try to cruise and end up wasting their gifts. Bruce didn't mind working on his poetry, and while he rarely changed direct criticisms of poems proffered, he sometimes did embody the critique and employed them in later poems he wrote. But, Bruce's most *famous* poems, in terms of those talked of in the UPG and other circles where Bruce was known as a poet, were those that were featured on Cosmoetica's UPG page: http://www.cosmoetica.com/UPG.htm.

Jess and I, however, were not the only folks leaving the Twin Cities. Inside of 6 months of our departure, Bruce was the only original and core UPGer left in the Twin Cities, and from what he told me, he bounced around from bad poetry group to bad poetry group, often lamenting that none of them came close to the UPG in terms of quality poems and criticism, even as Bruce often fucked up his own poetry in order to please whatever groups and people he interacted with—a negative trait of *people-pleasing* that led to the later bowdlerization of his great novel *Cityboy*, by a vanity press he hired in the 2010s, as well as an incident at a UPG meeting, wherein the idiotic owner of the place where Bruce worked, the Steeple People thrift store, where we held the group quite often, illegally towed one of my cars after years of allowing UPGers to park in its parking lot. We sued the owner and easily won the towing costs back, but Bruce was too scared to testify that we had always been allowed to park there after the owner threatened his job. Over the years since that incident, Bruce expressed regret for not having stood up and told the truth, but we forgave him, as this was simply how Bruce was. It was also one of the reasons, aside from poetry and personal issues, why Bruce admired me—I stood up for things and to bullies, even if it cost me; which it often did in art, life, and work. Bruce did not really stand up for things, and this was why and how many people, in and out of the arts, took advantage of his nice people-pleasing nature, and occasional inability to process things in a normal manner.

This brings me back to the subject of the vanity press Bruce got involved with late in his life. They bowdlerized his great novel, *Cityboy,* to such a degree that Jessica and I will have to restore the novel to its original state, as the third step in establishing Bruce's literary merit and reputation, after the release of these *Selected Poems*, and his *Final Poems*. The mutilation started with the novel's title, which changed from *Cityboy* to *City Boy*, for no real reason, and which is especially egregious considering the main character's identity is totally tied up in the city of Minneapolis, hence the merged word and title makes sense. Even the subtitle given the book, as *A Memoir*, is wrong, as the book is clearly not a memoir, but a novel, a *roman a clef*, for the main character is named John Argent, Jr., not Bruce Ario, and while there are many parallels to Bruce's real life in his novel, there are also significant parts, perhaps a third of the book, that are fiction, as told to me by Bruce himself. Then there is a bad opening paragraph added before the original ending, which utterly mutes the original version's great, poetic, and gripping start—typical of the edits and additions that altered Bruce's very vision of the work. There are numerous other additions that are typical MFA hackery, such as explaining too many things in the narrative to make obvious things *painfully* obvious, overdescriptions just for the need to '*unpack*'—an MFA weasel word—a work for the illiterate; things wholly added to the original great novel, things which often mute Bruce's clarion voice and genericize the work, including, especially, the memorable beginnings and ends of many chapters. The book's last page, mirroring the bowdlerized start, has even more larding on of unneeded and generic writing that makes the original version's great ending something far less than it was. Fortunately, the same PC that unlocked Bruce's *Final Poems* also led me to an annotated text by the vanity press that included specific changes guided by constant references to (*ugh!*) the wretched and inane *Chicago Manual of Style*.

Over the last few years of his life, Bruce, in talks and emails, often regretted letting the vanity press destroy his great novel. Jessica recalls that Bruce once said, 'I don't know how I let them talk me into changing my book,' to which I comically replied, 'They used words, Bruce, they used words;' only to have Bruce sigh in disgust of himself and his people-pleasing nature. Jess and I will, though, right this great literary wrong done to Bruce, just as this essay and book will right the wrong of Bruce's poetic neglect. But, let me be clear, as great a novel as *Cityboy* is, it is Bruce's poetic corpus and place in world poetry history that is the foundation of his literary output and reputation. Above all, Bruce was a poet first—a great poet. All the rest is, as the saying goes, just icing on the cake. This book will ultimately and definitively rest on my making the case that Bruce Ario is one of not only the English language's greatest poets, but one of the world's greatest poets.

To return to the issue of the UPG's end, though, after the lawsuit, the UPG started rotating venues between participants' personal homes and public places, like coffee shops and book stores, and this fact also led to the eventual end of the group; not to mention that from 1995 to 2003, the UPG's lifespan, poetry went from one of its periodic upswings in cultural consciousness back to near oblivion; hence there were less people writing poetry about town.

After we moved, Bruce stayed in touch with Jess (whom he always had a crush on) and me via my Cosmoetica email list, and, later, Skype. A few times I did video interviews and shows with Bruce for my Cosmoetica (https://tinyurl.com/2smepk5a) and Alex Sheremet's automachination (https://tinyurl.com/3k54mpjy) YouTube channels. Bruce was, in a sense, always there in our lives, as if just around the corner—and yes, as he aged he put on some weight and his posture and intellect suffered a bit. Fortunately, after the debacle of the vanity press's horrid editing of *Cityboy*, Bruce seemed to realize that he was not the person capable of making literary decisions about his work, and, along with his religion, this was paramount to him, as Bruce rightly viewed himself as a representative of not only himself but of all mentally ill people. He desperately wanted his work to survive him, to show that the mentally ill could be productive citizens, and he knew that, as I once said, *I would take better care of his work than he could*. Bruce therefore made me his literary executor, rather than a family member.

This choice proved all too true and cogent when, on the 6th day of August 2022, Bruce somehow fell in his own condominium, hit his head, likely on his radiator, bathtub, or bath counter, according to his kin, and never saw the light of living again. Ironically, when I later hired a computer tech to get into Bruce's PC I not only found more poems (as elaborated upon in other parts of this essay) but a June 2022 bill for new glazed bathroom floor tiles—meaning, more shiny and slippery than most, as opposed to the tiles Jess and I have, which are rough and slip resistant; ironically meaning Bruce likely slipped and died on a new bathroom floor less than 2 months after paying for its installation. The 6th was a Saturday, and the next day, a Sunday, Bruce did not show up to his beloved church service at the Hennepin Avenue United Methodist Church. The day after that he failed to show up at his mailroom job with Tasks Unlimited. Bruce's surviving family was contacted and they, and the property representatives, entered his condo and found Bruce's body, as well as a very disheveled living quarters, accompanied by a foul smell. This led to the building owner coming in and tossing stuff, as he had the condo cleaned. It is unknown what, if any, of Bruce's artistic works, may have been purged in the initial cleanup. What was left of Bruce's work—written, typed, digital, and his desktop PC—was sent to me by his brothers. I already had a good bulk of Bruce's most valued writings sent to me by him on CD and online. In looking over these poems, which ranged from doggerel to great, I again feel I was always in Bruce's presence. Not that he was ever far—just an email or phone call away; but in these poems many things I thought about Bruce were confirmed, while others were revelations.

But, before I get too far afield from the man, himself, I reprint herein the obituary published in the Minneapolis Star-Tribune (https://tinyurl.com/bdcc37cz) and other venues, by his family, with minor alterations:

> Bruce Dwayne Ario, age 67, of South Minneapolis, died unexpectedly after falling at home on August 6, 2022. Bruce was born on April 29, 1955 in Virginia, MN, the second of four boys born to Frank and Georgette Ario.
>
> Bruce spent most of his childhood in the Washburn High School neighborhood. Bruce graduated from the University of MN with an economics degree in 1978 and attended the University of Minnesota Law School, though his struggles with mental illness prevented him from completing his final year.
>
> Bruce lived a remarkable life despite his illness. After a traumatic brain injury in 1979, caused by a serious car accident, Bruce struggled to find appropriate mental health services and went without effective treatment and medication for five years, during which he endured bouts of homelessness while pursuing his legal studies. He hit bottom in 1984 and finally found the therapy and medication he needed to turn his life around.
>
> Bruce went on to become both a beneficiary and public advocate for Tasks Unlimited, where he led various work teams for the last 35 years of his life and won multiple awards, including the John K. Trepp Innovator of the Year Award in 2013 for 'creative thinking that carries on the spirit of the Fairweather philosophy to help people reclaim their lives from the limitations of mental illness.' He was a frequent public speaker for Tasks, NAMI, NASW, law enforcement, and other groups on how best to understand and support people with mental illness.
>
> In his spare time, Bruce wrote poetry, plays and novels (his four novels are available on Amazon), and frequently read from his work at local writer workshops. He also ran seven marathons in the 1990s, learned karate, managed a used clothing charity,

made mission trips to Haiti and India, and was a lay leader at the Hennepin Avenue United Methodist Church.

Bruce was still going strong when tragedy struck on August 6. Bruce struck his head and died shortly after posting this on social media: 'Greta Thunberg gives me hope.' His remains were cremated.

Bruce was beloved by his family and loved to write poems for birthdays and other family events. He is survived by three brothers, Joel (Diana), David, and Kevin (Paula), and six nieces and nephews. He was preceded in death by his parents, Frank and Georgette.

A memorial service will be held at Hennepin Avenue United Methodist Church, 511 Groveland Avenue, on Friday, August 26 with visitation at 10:30 AM and Service at 11:00 AM followed by a light lunch. Memorials preferred to Hennepin Avenue UMC or Tasks Unlimited. Condolences, memories, and photos welcome to the guestbook: startribune.com.

Note the typical way the most important and memorable part of Bruce's life is handled in the obituary: *In his spare time, Bruce wrote....* Of course, this is how such things go with artists. His family had no idea of Bruce's stature as a poet and writer, good nor bad, and had I not been appointed his literary executor, who knows what would have become of Bruce's great verse, and other works of varying quality that avoided possible trashing? That stated, my dealings with his kin have been positive, and hopefully when this book is available for purchase they will recognize that Bruce is as intimately tied to his time and place as any other artist has ever been tied to a time and place.

Bruce Ario is THE Minneapolis Poet!

Art, writing, and poetry, especially in his ario form, is THE most important thing Bruce ever did. Yes, Bruce was a good man, and religious, but no one would know of him for that alone. His art, though, is his immortality, and I will demonstrate this in the bulk of this essay. In fact, **all** great artists become their art. Many a man has been good and religious. Many a man has been the fan of a pop icon—in Bruce's case, Bob Dylan. But only Bruce invented the ario. Bruce made up a *de facto* 10-line free verse sonnet form I dubbed the *ario*, which narratively often mirrors the English (or Shakespearean) sonnet form with its 3-3-3-1 vs. 4-4-4-2 stanza line formatting. In a sense, this unique form may one day even prove as important a technical breakthrough in poetry as Walt Whitman's long lined breathiness which birthed all of Modern Poetry across the globe. More on the import of Bruce's poetry in a bit, though.

Bruce was not merely an artist, nor a victim of circumstances; he was also human. I have listed some of his flaws and foibles, and many of his poems written over about a 40-year period or so, display these. Bruce himself was not sure when he actually started writing poems and other genres. What was his first adult poetic effort is a mystery, but given what his obituary claims, and from what Bruce said to me and others, I am pretty sure his start was after he got into therapy and off of living on the street. It is worth noting that Bruce had a rather dim view of the bulk of the mental health profession, as he felt many of his doctors (some court-appointed) were quacks, or cruel, or utterly uncaring; but he did what they said, more often than not, and he slowly recovered his sanity and semblance of well-being. Poetry was just a part of that part of his life. To his credit, though, poetry was NOT just therapy, as it is in many other bad poets' works. Bruce transcended *art as therapy* into art—*great art*—ever so slowly, and with a resistance from within, as well as without.

While there may have been some germs of Bruce's verse before 1984 (hence why this book's *Selected Poems* are dated back to 1980, to be more inclusive), I think 1984 was the first year Bruce would look at himself as both a Born Again Christian and a poet. But, Bruce was almost 30 when he took off into the arts. That he achieved greatness at all is incredibly rare, especially given his addictions and mental woes, and that he did so with such a late start is alone is even more remarkable as anyone who has been as immersed in the arts as I have for almost four decades knows that most artists peak in their early to mid-30s, and then soon drop off and just repeat themselves till death. Bruce, however, got *better* with age. As I mentioned, virtually every steady and long-term member of the UPG did improve, with the best of their work occurring during or after the UPG years. While Bruce's insecurities and damnable desire to please others often led him to allow a work—*novel, play, poem*—to be bowdlerized by a know-nothing, he also was writing more and more small collections of verse, and poems of quality. Yet Bruce could write a great ario, then write 20 pieces of doggerel in a row, and not fully understand why one was great and the others terrible and trite.

This *Selected Poems*, therefore, is unlike any other published in that I will use this book as Walt Whitman wanted: to help build great audiences for great poetry—Bruce's, and hopefully others. The poems are divided into 4 sections: great arios (46), great non-arios (8), publishable arios (265), and publishable non-arios (59), for a total of 378 poems. I have decided that, since the poems Bruce sent me digitally when he appointed me literary executor (as well as those written in ink, magic marker, in notebooks, on old computer printouts from the 80s and 90s, and so forth, tallying 800 or more poems) work so well, this will be his *Selected Poems* volume of quality poems. The aforementioned later poems I discovered on his PC will be a *Final Poems* volume, making the total 576 poems, 63 of which are great.

The poems herein are not arranged via collection nor date of writing—hard to pin down specifically, other than broad eras based on the medium the poems were written on, but by movements of theme, style, and other things. They are generally in this volume due to quality, although a few merely *passable* poems are included to give the reader a broader view of Bruce's life, thus aiding in the appreciation of the rest of the poems, as well. No bad poems appear here, although there are clichés that are in poems that overcome or undermine them with subversive tactics—barely or well—in ways I will demonstrate.

As for the personal aspects the poems reveal, let me briefly speak of three aspects that I will go into greater detail in when I speak of the poems themselves. All of them revolve around sex. As far as I know, Bruce was wholly heterosexual, but even before his accident he had a rough go of it with the opposite sex. This manifested itself in Bruce's fetish for women's nylon legwear. From what I recall, Bruce, at his low ebb, sometimes indulged in pornography and prostitution, and this led him to the discovery of women's nylons. Not that he was indulging in transvestism, he just, as he said several times to me and Jess, liked the feel of nylons on his legs. The funny thing is Bruce would always say this and look at us and then look down or away. But we never judged him on this harmless indulgence. As he aged, and we had long accepted Bruce's fetish with no care of it, Bruce seemed to still feel queasy over it, as if it was a personal failing he was eternally vexed by; yet he still wrote poems of it, which he knew would be in the public domain. He would send an email or post about it—and other personal and familial matters—on social media, then remove them. He would write me long and odd emails trying to psychologically justify the fetish, as if it mattered to me. It did matter to Bruce, though. Maybe he was able to quell his urges only by explaining or damning them to people he knew would not label him a pervert or worse.

During the same era that he developed his women's nylons fetish, Bruce also got into far more troubling things: drugs, alcohol, and prostitutes—no pun intended. He spoke of these endeavors sometimes openly, and other times with more circumspection. Seeing his final years, and how Bruce's body and mind seemed to decay, I am certain that these things ever affected Bruce, even as he was drug-free and sober the last few decades of his life. These things affect the body adversely, and even later abstinence cannot heal the damage caused completely. I think of the death of writer and Nuyorican Slam Poet, Maggie Estep (1963 – 2014), an old friend and acquaintance from my New York art days, by heart attack at just 50 years old, and recall all the alcohol and drugs she took in her youth, see later photos of her bodily decay, aged far beyond her years, and know it likely played a large role in her premature death by weakening her body and heart, even as other so-called friends and acquaintances glossed over such failings. I got the same deteriorating vibes in mind and body from my last few years of dealing with Bruce.

Then, after finding poetry and God—and I will maintain that THAT is the correct order for Bruce's life's latter half's import— there came his great loneliness. Bruce's poems, often his best, qualitatively, subjectwise, and so forth, are dominated by *aloneness*, *lonesomeness*, and *loneliness*, especially in his best poems, and often tucked neatly under more seemingly joyous themes. This abject, sexual, and existential loneliness is embodied in a publishable ario called *In The Bushes*, wherein mid-poem, Bruce declares: *I haven't had sex for 30 years. / There has to be a happy medium.* Having known and spoken with Bruce, I feel this was not just a poetic statement, as this is a later poem, and its sentiment just *feels* true, however sad. Moreso than sexlessness, though, Bruce yearned for true and romantic love. Was his fervor for religious love a substitute for sexual/romantic love? Almost assuredly. Even Bruce would likely admit so.

I stated above that aloneness, lonesomeness, and loneliness dominated Bruce's best poems. Ironically, yet predictably, God dominated his worst and unpublishable poems—well, God and women. Despite being a Born Again Christian, Bruce was not a great formally religious poet in the manner of John Donne (1572 – 1631), Gerard Manley Hopkins (1844 – 1889), nor Countee Cullen (1903 – 1946). He was, instead, a great *spiritual poet*, and much of what masques as religious poetry in his oeuvre is quite secular in its approach to what many would term *sacred*. His spiritual poems are generally more sacred and much better wrought than his overtly religious Christian poems.

Yet, through it all, in most ways, Bruce Ario lived, he thrived, through terrible times; be it what his brain inflicted on him, what addictions left him, or through the long decades of lovelessness—at least in the sexual realm. I know that Bruce would have preferred a life as a husband and father, even at the cost of most or the whole of his artistic achievement, but that was not to be. For the culture of the world, at least, I am grateful Bruce lived the life he lived, even at the personal costs I have mentioned. The truth is that the car accident likely irrevocably altered Bruce. Without it, and the changes wrought to his brain, I fully believe the world would not recall Bruce as a poet, much less a great one, for he would *never have been* a poet. The very thing that robbed Bruce of any chance at personal joy and fulfillment made him an instrument and also a creator for art's and poetry's power. The cognitive limits the accident forced upon Bruce made him utilize other ways to see and think of all the cosmos offered—and some of them were *better* ways! Call it what you will, but that instinct or intuition came to the forefront and made him hit and miss in verse, because reason was less important—yet when he hit, he really hit it!

In some ways, Bruce was a living embodiment of the term that English poet John Keats (1795 – 1821) proffered: Negative Capability. Generally thought of as the way Keats described it as '....being in uncertainties, mysteries, doubts, without any irritable reaching after fact and reason,' I have refined the term to mean what is more explicit in art: *when an artist is able to see connections between things and ideas that most people, those sans creativity, cannot, yet which, after being pointed out, seem obviously connected to even the least creative, as if the connection had always been made.*

This was Bruce. He may have personally lost the battles of life, but the poetic war was now his to win, and this book is the study of how Bruce did win, and how even his personal losses better all who read this book.

Yes, Bruce Ario thrived in the arts in ways he could not in life.

This book is the first step in making his art thrive after his death.

And Bruce did thrive in the arts by becoming something else I neglected to mention in this essay's opening. He became a weirdo. Well, specifically a *weirdo poet*, and in a bit I shall explain that and compare him with other notable weirdo artists and poets.

But first, and most importantly, it is important to take a look at some of the poems that plant Bruce Ario's flag on a soil that only a few dozen others in human history can claim.

That of simply *great poet*.

Excelsior!

The Poems

Let us now look at the body of Bruce Ario's poetic corpus, and how and why I can easily make a claim for Bruce's greatness as a poet, and likely his place, at minimum as a Top 20 to 25 English language poet of all time.

But, *how* to determine that? First one must qualitatively reckon whether or not a work of art is great or not, and I'll do that in a bit. Second, one must then compare such things as the number of great poems, their length and heft—after all, a great book length poem bests a great long poem, which bests a page or two length poem, which bests a sonnet, which bests a haiku, etc. Why, because it is harder to sustain quality over longer and longer works. This does not mean that a great haiku might not contain an image or metaphor better than a book-length poem's, but it will only have one or two versus possibly dozens of hundreds in the book-length poem. After all, greatness is not just a measure of quality but scope—a term and idea at home in Bruce's poems. Lastly, there must be a diversity of approaches and themes and techniques to one's art, for diversity helps eliminate an artist simply repeating themselves. Hence, quality, quantity, and diversity are the three hallmarks of greatness.

In this book of 378 poems, I state that 54 of Bruce's poems (46 arios and 8 non-arios) are easily gleaned great poems. I have applied a very strict and fine measure of this, and, if anything, I have undercounted his great verse, just to be on the safe side. I have done the same with my corpus.

In terms of all the other great traditionally published poets I have read, the most are the 71 great poems I would claim for Rainer Maria Rilke (1875 – 1926); 3 or 4 of them being written in French, and the rest in German—a feat of being bilingually great that sets Rilke apart from others. Of course, this is looking at translations into English, so there is a good deal of variability. I often give foreign language poets the critical benefit of the doubt, maybe adding 10-15% of qualitative grading to the translated poem on my classic elementary school grading system of 0-100, with anything 64 or under being bad to terrible poetry (aka poetastry or doggerel), 65-69 being passable or ok poetry, 70-74 being solid poetry, 75-79 being good poetry, 80-84 being very good poetry, 85-89 being excellent poetry, 90 to 94 being near great poetry, and 95 and above being great poetry. 100 would be impossible on this scale, but the numeric progression is not linear. Like the TV franchise *Star Trek* does with its warp speed numeration, it is harder to go from a 94 to a 95 rating than from, say, 68 to 85, or the like. That is because the closer one gets to greatness and its ineffability, the harder each little step becomes. Also, in translations, the translator matters, as Russian poet Boris Pasternak (1890 – 1960) has several translators whose translations of his work come nowhere near greatness, and some who make him shine. Hence, there is well more subjectivity in translated literature than other art forms.

Back to Rilke and his 71 great poems. After that mark, there are poets like Walt Whitman (1819 – 1892), Wallace Stevens (1879 – 1955), and my wife, Jessica Schneider, that have in the 40 to 60 poem range; then the likes of Hart Crane (1899 – 1932), Carl Sandburg (1878 – 1967), Robinson Jeffers (1887 – 1962), Robert Frost (1874 – 1963), and Sylvia Plath (1932 – 1963) with 25 to 40, depending, as well as other poets with up to two dozen. Again, foreign language poets are hard to rate on this scale when talking of their translations into English, and as mentioned I tend to give them more a benefit of the doubt than native English language poets.

Among poets whose names will appear later in this essay, William Shakespeare (1564 – 1616) has 8 to 12 great sonnets, and, if one takes some of his dramas' soliloquies as stand-alone dramatic poetic monologues, one can get him into the 20 to 25 great poem range as well. John Donne is also in the 20 to 30 range. Emily Dickinson (1830 – 1886), however, has maybe a similar 8-12 great poems as Shakespeare, without the possible bonus of monologues as poems. Yet Shakespeare and Dickinson are alike in another way and that is all 1800+ of Dickinson's poems, and all 154 of Shakespeare's sonnets, are extremely limited in range and scope. Both poets basically wrote 7 or 8 types of poems over and over again, sort of the way Hermann Hesse (1877 – 1962) wrote several versions of *Demian*-like novels before he wrote *Demian*. Whether they wrote the best version first and then tried and failed to repeat the success, and wrote poems that were like Xerox copies of a copy, or whether they wrote a promising but flawed poem and then tried a dozen versions of a similarly themed poem until they finally got it right, is of no real matter. Both poets, while arguably great poets, are vastly overrated. Shakespeare was quickly trumped by Donne in the 17th Century, whose first real rival for greatest English language poet would be Whitman, 200 years later. Shocking though this may seem in our Age of Bardolatry, Donne was poetically better than Shakespeare in every way—musically, intellectually, emotionally, and literarily. The best phrasing of this reality was given to me by a young Irish woman and poet I know named Laura Woods, who stated that the difference between Donne and Shakespeare is that one never gets the sense from Donne that the words he uses do not flow naturally. His words are integral and organic, but with Shakespeare there is often the sense that he is just choosing words to pad out a line; be it for the sake of iambic pentameter (although classical meter does not exist, as I have long argued in my essay, *Politics & Theory: Robinson Jeffers & The Metric Fallacy*: http://www.cosmoetica.com/S2-DES2.htm) or just to say *something*, or meet a syllabic count.

Similarly, little-known Portland, Oregon poet Hazel Hall (1886 – 1924) has a similar or bit greater number of great poems as Dickinson, but with a vastly smaller corpus, which thus poses the question of how much do we take into account a poet's lesser work, and do we count juvenilia at all?, as someone like Plath can count 3 or 4 poems of her juvenilia with her greatest poems. Is a poet with

10 great poems out of a corpus of 50 or 60 published poems greater than a poet with 10 great poems out of 300? 1000? And what of the layers below? If there is a poet with 20 great poems and a steep drop off in quality, is a poet with 10 or 12 great poems, but many more near great or excellent poems better or greater than the poet with more great poems but a huge cliff? One need only look at T.S. Eliot (1888 – 1965) and his canon. As influential as he was, he has maybe 5 or 6 great poems, then a steep decline into doggerel and near-doggerel. Does the influence of his few great poems outweigh, say, the 10 or 20 or more great poems of now forgotten poets like Kenneth Patchen (1911 – 1972) or Robert Hayden (1913 – 1980)? And does a poet with no or maybe 1 or 2 great poems, but uniformly good to excellent to near great poetry, that numbers in the hundreds, like Mark Van Doren (1894 – 1972), best a poet with 10 to 15 great poems and an erratic quality to the rest of his corpus? And I won't even get into trying to separate the Visionary from the Creationary from the Functionary types of intellect in life and the arts, such as: is a Creationary great poet like James Emanuel (1921 – 2013) lesser than a Visionary poet like Plath or Crane, even if they may have a comparable number of great poems?

Years ago I wrote of this and have since charted the issues it brings in determining quality (http://www.cosmoetica.com/D1-DES1.htm):

....the human mind has 3 types of intellect. #1 is the Functionary- all of us have it- it is the basic intelligence that IQ tests purport to measure, & it operates on a fairly simple add & subtract basis. #2 is the Creationary- only about 1% of the population has it in any measurable quantity- artists, discoverers, leaders & scientists have this. It is the ability to see beyond the Functionary, & also to see more deeply- especially where pattern recognition is concerned. And also to be able to lead observers with their art. Think of it as Functionary^2. #3 is the Visionary- perhaps only 1% of the Creationary have this in measurable amounts- or 1 in 10,000 people. These are the GREAT artists, etc. It is the ability to see farther than the Creationary, not only see patterns but to make good predictive & productive use of them, to help with creative leaps of illogic (Keats' Negative Capability), & also not just lead an observer, but impose will on an observer with their art. Think of it as Creationary^2 , or Functionary^3.

So where does Bruce stand in comparison to some of these poets? Well, I stated he had 63 great poems (54 in this work) by my stringent standards, so maybe he has an equal to greater number of poems than Whitman or Stevens, and maybe even bests Rilke's 71? It's possible since Rilke was given that 10-15% boost, as one can tell by subject matter and word choice and setting choice if a poem that's merely very good or excellent in translation is likely great in its original language. But, even if Bruce has 75 great poems, in reality, is he greater than Rilke? Well, Rilke was bilingually great—Bruce was not. Bruce has no poems, herein nor in his unpublished poems, that go for more than a page, while Rilke has long poems like the *Duino Elegies*, Stevens has many longer philosophical poems, while Whitman has many huge *Songs*, and Jeffers a number of huge book-length dramatic poems. So, just how many small poems and arios equal Crane's *The Bridge*? Or Whitman's *Song Of Myself*, and so on? Because, on a counting sheet of discrete works of art, Bruce's 63 great poems is likely greater than those I mentioned above, and Top 10 in the English language, amongst poems published by major outlets, and easily Top 20 to 25 in global poetry annals.

Let us let that sit in the readers' minds for now so I can turn to something else. I have sketched out how I view and rank poems and poets, so let me turn to a bit of information about these 378 poems selected within.

Bruce sometimes had a handwritten poem version, a typed one, one on a WORD document, and in those cases it was easy to see the final version, and usually this was the best version. But not always, so sometimes I would pick the best version of a line and add it to the best version of the poem if that were lacking it. But that was rare. More often I would do that if had two poem versions that differed but there was no sure date on each. In general, I corrected bad choices Bruce made, although, in truth, Bruce rarely changed poems once typed or printed up. You could see changes in handwritten versions, but rarely once those poems were printed. And most of the criticisms that were given by UPG members were not taken up by Bruce—even as he would often bowdlerize his own work to please an idiot in other venues. However, the few times Bruce changed a poem after UPG criticisms came when he listened to my advice. Hence, I felt safe that Bruce would 99% of the time agree with the few changes I made to get a best version of his poem. If not, I would not have been chosen to caretake his literary legacy. As my wife, Jessica, often pointed out, Bruce was maybe the only true *first thought best thought* poet to ever be any good at any level, much less great. Many of the Beatniks who claimed such were liars and/or doggerelists and never practiced that—such was just bullshit mythologizing. Some folks claimed that Bruce did not know good from bad writing, and there is merit to this, but not in toto. Instinct over intellect would seem to have been Bruce's motto, but there *is* intellect—often great intellect—in his work, as well.

In short, I always went with the best version of poem, stanza, or line, save for a few poems where there were changes that went sideways. In those cases I left both versions in this book, as one can see below. And while quality was the overwhelming reason a poem made this book's cut or not, I did include a literal handful or so of just passable poems here because they were essential to Bruce's life experience and philosophy and not really bad poems of the sort we will see later when I compare Bruce's canon to published poems of others; they were just ok—see if you can find them.

The physical process was tedious, but I breezed through the choosing and editing of poems, as well arranging them in movements and order, much more quickly than in doing this essay because I am well-practiced in the construction of books, and less so in crusades to boost a friend's great art. I had to sort through 100s of typed poems, on WORD and like documents, some printed on old 1980s-style computer printouts, others typed on an actual typewriter, handwritten into notebooks; even some poems written in magic marker! Many were not good poems, even doggerel, while others were just fragments. I read through many little chapbook-length collections of poems, as well as a whole manuscript of over 70 poems dedicated to apples—only 2 of which made it into this book.

As I mentioned, the number of lost poems and works, due to Bruce's organizational lack, and the posthumous cleaning out of his condominium, may have resulted in my dealing with only a portion of Bruce's actual work. Whether that is 50% or 75% or 90% of his actual work, well, I cannot say, but Jessica recalls the very first ario poem she ever read (titled *What Shadow?*) that she says I thought was an excellent or great ario. While the title seems familiar, the poem—apparently about a lake, according to Jess's much better memory than mine—is not in the printed nor digital poems I have received, and unless they are on the desktop PC Bruce's brother mailed me, it is unfortunately likely lost forever. It is just as likely there were a few 100 poems, at minimum that were either lost at his death or in the years before, due to Bruce's failing memory and general slovenly lifestyle. Were I to guess, I'd say I dealt with about 700-800 fully formed poems of his, and he likely had 1000 or so poems, so, one way or another about half the life's output that Emily Dickinson had, with a 4 to 6 times or more success rate at hitting greatness.

Putting aside qualitative and stylistic issues, and sticking to just punctuation and other technical matters as enjambment, rhyme, alliteration, and so forth, I generally left all of Bruce's punctuation as is, as Bruce was hell mell in such; unless there was an obvious misspell or wrong punctual usage. If Bruce had punctuation, I left it in. If a poem or a line lacked punctuation, I added none. I was not going to do to Bruce's work, after death, what the damnable vanity press did to *Cityboy*, nor what Dickinson's first editors and publishers did to her poems after her death. If I changed anything punctually or spelling-wise they were obvious errors on Bruce's part.

Overall I was very happy that Bruce's great poems were well more than I expected, even though I knew he likely had 15 to 20 minimum, and the number of quality poems from good upwards to near great were also more than I hoped for. In fact, I was thinking if Bruce had 60 to 80 total poems of quality it would be a strong argument I could make for his overall greatness as a poet. That I ended up with many times that, well....

As for formal poetry—Bruce basically had his ario, and a lone haiku. There were no sonnets, villanelles, nor sestinas to be reckoned with, to pick three of the most popular poem forms.

Regarding the ario form itself, here is how Bruce described it in regards to a small collection he put on Amazon called *Coming Around* (https://tinyurl.com/2kvbn6t7):

> I write 10 line verse in three stanzas with a final one line ending also known by some as the 'Ario'. The first stanza sets up the poem, the second stanza further develops it, the third stanza can raise questions, and the final line takes us off to space.

Bruce was not a formalist, at heart, and the ario form is only a lineal form, with great flexibility. Rhyme, alliteration (consonance or assonance), metrics, even the use of bolded or italicized words, are almost nonexistent in Bruce's repertoire.

Then there were poems that were untitled. Some were truly sans any title, while others had the title *Untitled*. The latter poems I left with the *Untitled* title, and the rest I had explanations bracketed as title.

This all said, while Bruce was relentless in his use of the first-person singular 'I', and that 'I' was almost always Bruce himself, he was no navel-gazer, nor poet that wrote only in a Confessional and/or Personalist style. Bruce was well-acquainted with high and low art, as in this publishable ario that references both Wallace Stevens's *Thirteen Ways Of Looking At A Blackbird*, as well as Alfred Hitchcock's film, *The Birds*, based on the Daphne du Maurier tale:

Forget About 13 Blackbirds

Thousands where I am by the bus.
This park levies fear in its trees
Where I wonder if I'll be attacked.

Hitchcock's not around
So I wonder what's up with these birds
In this nocturnal gathering.

I've been to baseball games, seen crowds...
But there's no food here...is there?
Still they sit

Eerie like being stalked or something.

Note how the speaker defangs the apparent threat he recalls from birds and their ways by conflating the scene with food from a baseball game, then ends with the simple statement of what the birds are doing, and then the line and stanza break that states something, or rather equates it with what we've already been given in the rest of the poem. Then, the title comes back and the Stevens reference may be more of a self-invocation against fear by the speaker to try and block out the 13 blackbirds that may be creeping him out, as in,

'Forget about them, forget what is happening,' as the speaker turns inward to try and block out the eerie world.

Bruce could also dig down into pop art. Check out the below publishable ario that invokes Charles Schulz's *Peanuts* comic strip character Charlie Brown's famed failure with being able to get a kite in the air without it being eaten by a kite-eating tree:

Brace Against The Wind

You stood, a tree forming
Sending roots, branches, bark
Like a residence of Earth

You basement in a storm
An ice over water
Glue onto the paper airplane I was

Caught a leaf
Not resting
Until

The kite was rolled home.

Yes, this poem does not invoke the comic strip trope overtly, and it's about someone trying to root themselves against some coming crisis, but that end image is clarion for a boy from Minnesota, be it Schulz or Bruce.

Similarly, the great ario below invokes Charlie Brown's most noteworthy exclamation of exasperation, even as it undermines the self-pitying tone by making the actual words of the title into a simple modifier of emotion:

Good Grief

A famous singer who I respected said,
'Good work is never done until the mourning comes'
And I believe it was 'mourning' not 'morning'.

I went through my boyhood never feeling grief
It was all laughter and on to the next laugh
Until my Grannie died and returned to me as an angel.

Grief, grieving, grove, grieven, grievous

Good, better, cleansing, reflection, solitude
Water, tears, sleep, music, maturity, God

Never ceasing, carry me to the next day.

Note the play with language itself, the subtle turns by how words are modified in tense and usage, and then we end up with an invocation of God that is surprisingly utilitarian and pedestrian—one of the best uses of that word in Bruce's corpus precisely because it is not cluttered by all the religious baggage it usually lugs. Also, the enjambment, sans punctuation, at the end of line 9, really shows how choices as seemingly small as that can add duplicity to the meaning of a line, or even a whole poem.

And grief was, as we shall see, a large part of Bruce's poetic work.

Another comic strip that is invoked offhandedly by a great last line and image is *Calvin And Hobbes*, in the publishable ario below. It is the rare poem of Bruce's whose title is set in quotation marks. It does not really need to be, but as the bulk of the poem occurs in the percipient's mind as he rides and looks out of a bus, well, it may be an internal invocation from a different part of the speaker's subconscious:

'I'll Take That Bus'

Drifts of snow between the forgotten spring
And my soul heartened knowing it can't go on
As a winter intruding on my warmth.

A vehicle is able to maneuver the ice
Roughly cracking the cold block by block
In my bus as it tours winter wonderland.

Me? I'm safe I guess behind the glass window
Perched in my observatory
Packing, packing, packing

A snowball that is never thrown.

As seen, Bruce was not disinclined to take on higher arts, as well. The below great ario, one of many poems featuring buses, has a distinct Edward Hopper-like feel to it. One can easily imagine this nighttime scene being painted by the American master, and its human beings black-eyed as any of his own canvas's inhabitants. Interestingly, this is one of the rare great arios that was long pre-UPG, and likely dated from the late 1980s to the early 1990s, proving that Bruce was not merely a product of all the great poetic minds and critiques of others. Sometimes his dart tosses nailed absolute bull's-eyes:

Another Night Coming Home

Out of the deli
After a meeting
To a busstop.

It's ten o'clock
Been going since six this morning
I'm yawning under a streetlight.

The cars scurry down the road
Storekeepers leave their stores
Police walk the beat.

The busstop grows crowded.

This poem is an absolute masterpiece of simplicity. It is wholly dependent on the poesy of images, and juxtaposing prose lines, as there is nary a hint of alliteration nor rhyme, nor grand metaphor, and yet....it plays like a mini-film noir and ends at the moment just before whatever is bound to happen will happen, and then makes that moment the thing at the center of why the poem exists. Having known Bruce well, I can virtually guarantee that this is the sort of poem that probably came to Bruce after its real-life experience, and he just wrote it down inside of a minute, then put it on a pile and mostly forgot about it. Pre-UPG, this was the way most of his poems were crafted, and, in fact, most of them post-UPG as well.

The publishable ario below also touches upon pop culture, in the form of a 20th and 21st Century mouthwash's mention—yes, *Scope* mouthwash!—and the word *scope* has a distinct place in Bruce's canon, but this is its only turn as a pop cultural referent.

Rocks And Stars

Get that stone out of your pocket

And see if you can skip it on the river.
You're too young to be a rock.

Befuddle someone else's mind
With a piece of pie
Or a glimpse of a star whether

Human or celestial.
Your scope isn't a mouthwash
Because you can chart a bigger question

And you can skip off the river to the sky.

Of course, this poem is loaded with pop culture, aside from the mouthwash. The very title invokes the play off of fame and being a *rock star*, and the opening and closing images invoke a bevy of classic Americana, from Mark Twain's Mississippi River based prose works, to the opening scenes to the introduction to the classic TV sitcom, *The Andy Griffith Show*, to even something like Norman Maclean's *A River Runs Through It*.

This is one of those poems that just misses greatness for me, and I'd rate it a near great poem, but I would not put up much of an argument against it as a great ario, in the vein I mentioned re: my own critical stringency, so now is as good enough of a time to use this as an example as to my rating of it.

Below I will give some examples of how Bruce inverts a poem's worth of clichés—truly bad clichés if they were naked—and sometimes even makes such a poem soar into greatness: a feat that is literarily fantastic. In this poem, what is layered upon is not a raft of banalities but a mass of images that are variations on a theme, something that is an excellent thing as presented, but not as impressive as when actual clichés redeem the other clichés in a work by the cognitive dissonance created in their plays off of each other, thus producing a form of Negative Capability in the work.

But, there is not only Keatsian Negative Capability at work in many of Bruce's best poems, but another factor at play, limned by another poet who, like Keats, died prematurely. That of French poet Arthur Rimbaud (1854 – 1891) and derangement.

According to Rimbaud:

A poet makes himself a visionary through a long, boundless, and systematized disorganization of all the senses. All forms of love, of suffering, of madness; he searches himself, he exhausts within himself all poisons, and preserves their quintessences. Unspeakable torment, where he will need the greatest faith, a superhuman strength, where he becomes all men the great invalid, the great criminal, the great accursed—and the Supreme Scientist! For he attains the unknown! Because he has cultivated his soul, already rich, more than anyone! He attains the unknown, and if, demented, he finally loses the understanding of his visions, he will at least have seen them! So what if he is destroyed in his ecstatic flight through things unheard of, unnameable: other horrible workers will come; they will begin at the horizons where the first one has fallen!

Ok, aside from the childish melodrama, and the real-world silliness of someone making themselves a visionary rather than simply being one or not, the vastly overrated Rimbaud speaks in ways that later drug-fueled poets and other artists would of creativity coming about by not making the most of one's intellect and prowess, but deranging things. It's akin to the cliché that to be an artist one must revert to an infantile or childish state. Both are wrong, but the concept of actual *derangement*—not in the trite madness take on the word, but as in derangement being the opposite of *arrangement*—to be unarranged, well, this is valid, and something oft seen in Bruce's poetry. Bruce's derangement came, of course, due to his car accident and mental ills and addiction. It was likely born out of the same part of him that was able to engage in Negatively Capable ways with the world. This non-negative and non-pejorative sense of derangement can be seen in many of the leaps of illogic, real and Negatively Capable, that Bruce's poems bear.

Look at the poem's 3rd line:

Get that stone out of your pocket
And see if you can skip it on the river.
You're too young to be a rock.

It truly comes from some odd realm, as we get a literal seen, and injunction to act in an idyllic and romanticized way, and then line 3! How about stanza 2?

Befuddle someone else's mind

With a piece of pie
Or a glimpse of a star whether

Line 4 opens with an injunction, yet line 5 is hardly befuddling, unless the befuddling part is wondering how such a simple image *can* befuddle. And on and on.... And Bruce has even far weirder poems and images that derange really and Negatively Capably.

That all said, this poem comes awfully close to greatness, and if you want to include it and a dozen or so other poems I might consider near great, go ahead. I might join you in that opinion in a revised and/or later edition of this work.

I told you I was stringent!

The below publishable ario is also a recurring image and scene for Bruce, but this ario, while a solid poem, does not reach the heights of the prior poem, even as it deals with heights within. The expected images and metaphors—save for the cats and water one—simply do not energize, and the end is nothing daring nor memorable. Compared to Lawrence Ferlighetti's (1919 – 2021) Constantly Risking Absurdity (#15), on an acrobat, with its jaggered line placement and existential ending, well, it is simply more than what Bruce's poem offers:

                    And he
            a little charleychaplin man
                            who may or may not catch
                her fair eternal form
                            spreadeagled in the empty air
                    of existence

Bear Ferlinghetti's ending in mind compared to Bruce's:

The Tightrope

High above the artist walks
The thin path over the rope
Miles above the crowd.

Impressive the view,
But dangerous the height,
Still clasping a bar for balance.

Just the purpose

Is as far from his mind
As cats and water

Because he finds himself lost.

Yet, Ferlinghetti, for all his fame, and better poem in this thin
instance, was a fairly predictable writer with little depth. By showing
you this poem I want to make clear that I am not poetically
hagiographizing Bruce, but genuinely showing you why Bruce was a
great poet by offering some of the poems that were not great, to help
you realize why his great poems were great. One can often glean
more insight into great art by seeing the small failures of near great
art, as great art often seems hermetic—a thing only gods, not
mortals—can do. Pulling back the curtain and seeing the mechanics
of artistic failure is invaluable to an artist's improvement.

Bruce was, of course, mortal.

In the publishable non-ario below, Bruce humorously pokes fun at
his own mental health:

The Beatles

At some irrational point in my life
I wanted to be famous.
Who knows, maybe that's why I'm up here now.
Anyway, I think that one rock band
Really worked hard to share their fame with everybody
And make the concept of fame readily available
That being the Beatles.
They reveled in their fame
And took on their audiences face-to-face.
Their fame was so accessible
That on one occasion I thought they said,
'Bruce Ario'.
In my grandiosity I thought
'My God, the Beatles are singing about me.'
What they really said I found out later
Was 'impresario.'

This could almost be a prose poem, or proem, for its seeming flat
prose style, but the poem works because of the novel self-
deprecation and its explanation being so unique, which leads me into
an explanation of Bruce's last name, which is from the

German/Austrian, and is pronounced as **AIR-rio**, not **ARE-rio**, nor any other version, say with the short A vowel sound at the start. Bruce was very quick to point out a mispronunciation of his name, and the correct pronunciation factors into the poem's last line, as one of the top two pronunciations of *impresario* is as he pronounced his surname. That said, there is a family rift over the pronunciation of the name, being derived from the surname Ariowüstüs, according to Joel Ario, Bruce's older brother.

The great ario below also turns, and turns much higher than the prior poem, as Bruce names the names of those historical folks he admired, from names globally recognizable to those who are footnotes, then ascribes worth to them in the last line by connecting them to his name, thus connecting himself to them and their great or good achievements by stepping out into a third person view of himself. The penultimate line, which ends on what 99 times out of a 100 would be a bad enjambment—a hanging conjunction like *and*—is NOT bad as the very fusion of Bruce and his name with all the others lives up to the pause the break makes, and the choice of *and* actually is well chosen, as the reader's internal breath is bated by both line and stanza break, then—POW!

Running Through The Names

I've gotten to the point where I'm running through the names:
Abraham Lincoln, Christ, Mohammed, and Buddha, Anne Sexton.
Honest, spiritual, and poetic.

In time's eye they all seem to be One of an orchestra,
Part of a plan: Mark Twain, Hermann Hesse, Thomas Edison, Vincent
    Van Gogh.
They ease my situation: Margaret Mead, Betty Ford, Bob Dylan.

If only that dropping names was cool.
Harmon Killebrew, Mark Spitz, names that I've heard
Some tied to faces, places, and

Frames of reference for my Bruce Ario.

Note how Bruce actually connects the names. They are not directly tied *to* 'Bruce Ario,' the name, but to how he notes and connotes his very selfhood. This little twist psychologically opens up the poem and invites the reader in to decipher exactly why and how that will be done. This is the sort of little thing that becomes a big thing that is perhaps the lone thing holding back *Rocks And Stars* from being a great poem in my estimation; but is similar to the prosaic build up of *Another Night Coming Home*'s imagery that lifts it and *Running Through The Names* to greatness.

Let us now look at three great poems that involve Bruce's invoking the memory or image of his grandmother. Two are arios and the other not. Let us gauge the poems and then compare them to Hart Crane's *My Grandmother's Love Letters*:

Square World

Everything about America is so linear
Straight to the heart an arrow
slicing the cake into halves.

Even the doctors give shots
Through the skin paths
measured in centimeters.

Can you bum me a square?
He asked,
Not even knowing my name.

I made a big mistake when I gave away my grandmother's rocker.

To many, this ario may seem a hermetic poem, but it really is a throwback yearn for the America of yore, and is quite in sync with a later poem to be discussed, *1926*, by Weldon Kees (1914 – 1955). Looking at the title, the word *square* is used as an adjective, and while it can mean like the polygon, it presages several other meanings within. The first meaning the title could convey is *equitable*, as in *fair and square*, and this lingers over the poem as it longs for a lost time that was better. The first line then comes back to the polygonal meaning as it may be referencing American architecture, but linear, itself, can mean uncreative, thus making square mean *uncool* or *not hip*. Lines 2 and 3 drop *straight* and *halves* on the reader which reinforces the polygonal meaning, even as it implies America or the world is being divided or broken, be it fair or not. The second stanza's medical and mathematical references then make the word *square* conjure up the product of a number multiplied by itself. Then, in true scattershot Bruce fashion, line 7 wrenches the word, itself into something new. But what? To the young adult 21ˢᵗ Century reader the question asked—*Can you bum me a square?*—seems odd and hermetic. What the hell is he talking about? But given that, to this point, there seems to be a fracturing of the old order in the world and America, it seems obvious to an older reader that the square being bummed by a 'He' means that the speaker is being asked for some money to buy a good meal, likely by a bum—one who uses that very word as a verb in his query—another image that waxes nostalgic and harkens back to the Great Depression.

This odd encounter is then ended by a great line that seems to come out of nowhere, but is perfectly Negatively Capable: *I made a big mistake when I gave away my grandmother's rocker.* So, what the hell does this mean? The speaker is clearly catching up with the implications of a changing world by harking back to the past, and regretting giving away a piece of that past, especially one so tied to a now deceased and beloved relative.

Now, think of how many poems express such a sentiment, a regret of the passage of time, and think how many are as creative and effective, and damned well great as this one in that sentiment's expression.

Let us look again at a poem I earlier spoke of, and reuse it here because of its content rather than its expression of Bruce's pop cultural sensibilities.

Good Grief

A famous singer who I respected said,
'Good work is never done until the mourning comes'
And I believe it was 'mourning' not 'morning.'

I went through my boyhood never feeling grief
It was all laughter and on to the next laugh
Until my Grannie died and returned to me as an angel.

Grief, grieving, grove, grieven, grievous
Good, better, cleansing, reflection, solitude
Water, tears, sleep, music, maturity, God

Never ceasing, carry me to the next day.

The speaker's grandmother is now more familially mentioned, and line 6 (stanza 2) ends with what could be the end of the poem, as it seems pat, it seems done, it seems closed. Yet the poem then continues and reaches back into the idea of mourning, and the poem itself posits what purpose mourning serves—the culmination of good work. So, is stanza 3 the culmination? Is it positing grief as good, as connected to work? There are literally a dozen or more ways one might interpret the third stanza after the posits of the first 2 stanzas, but then line 10 slams in and the lack of punctuation after the ends of line 7 to 9 make sense as God is posited as never ceasing, and that equates with the never done posit of mourning, thus tying God with grief and work, and it all going on into the next day, and presumably every day after. The poem is kinetic in its listing of the many aspects and effects of grief in a world run by God. But the multiplicity of possible meanings really makes this poem multidimensional—a thing Bruce missed in most of his unpublishable poems that feature God, yet, as I posited earlier, is this really a religious poem or a spiritual poem?

I would argue the latter, for while God has the capital G, the things described in the poem, listed in the 3rd stanza, are all human universals, and not merely Christian artifacts of existences of quality. And all predicated on the speaker's grandmother.

Onward.

The 3rd grandmother poem of Bruce's I want to focus on is also a great one, but a non-ario:

Grandma

I talked to you last Friday night
And then you were gone.

The snow looks so white;
It's chilly outside.

No more phone calls...

No more

admonitions, stories, or worries... secrets.

All of my thoughts trail off
From a loving memory.
You were there when I needed you
You are where you need to be now.
 It isn't goodbye
 Because death turns to a new relationship...
     You are 98 years old and growing

                               upward.

                      touch

             light

        your

     trace

 I

Your gentle ways pass on...

I recall when Bruce brought this poem to the UPG and it is one of the few examples of where Bruce took something someone offered (me, in this case) and did not apply it to the poem under critique, but used it to formulate a poem that relied on line placement to a degree Bruce never did before nor after. I had mentioned to him of playing with the placement of lines in poems, as I sometimes did, and what came back, not long afterward, is simply a masterpiece of simple plainspokenness augmented by the placement of lines.

It reminds me of listening to a pitch-perfect voice singing simply and tenderly toward anything it holds in love and sacredness. The first 5 lines look like they might slip into banality, but the 'No more' off to the far right edge is the turn toward greatness.

And look at this line: 'Because death turns to a new relationship.' Understand its meaning and see how many ways other lesser poets in other lesser poems have said the same sentiments in far more trite ways. Note, too, that the speaker does NOT say that death turns 'into' a new relationship—i.e., that it has morphed; NO! The speaker states 'death turns to' that new relationship, as if death is outside of that relation. It is the literary equivalent of that scene in Stanley Kubrick's masterful *2001: A Space Odyssey*, near film's end, where David Bowman, played by Keir Dullea, ages and leaves earlier forms of himself behind, as older forms of himself look back on the younger forms of himself.

In essence, the statement and the ellipsis make plain that death is now discarded. Grandma (the *grandmother* of all 3 poems) is referred to differently in each poem—maybe it's several grandmothers, not just one? Nonetheless, after the ellipsis after 'relationship,' we see that this post-death relationship finds Grandma '98 years old and growing.' Has she died? Is this just the speaker's wish? Then we get the great upward lift of tracing her light upward. But here we get a multiplicity of meanings from this formatting. The word 'upward' has a period after it. Is this the last word dropping off from 'You are 98 years old and growing'? Or is it the end of the fragmented upward lifting line 'I trace your light touch'? Can that line, via lineal number be read as 'touch light your trace I,' with or without just a question mark missing? Does that represent a regression of the speaker to an earlier time—a sort of poetic rewinding of time and space?

Also note how the *You* representing Grandma, and the *I* representing the speaker, meet at the period. Is the period death itself? We know periods end things, and then a break of line and stanza for this exhalation, 'Your gentle ways pass on...' This could be so trite in a poem that is about one's dying grandmother, but after the poem that precedes it, it is a statement supercharged with meaning and genuine emotion.

And this is an important point in learning to defang seeming naked clichés by what is about them because clichés are all about not just their utterance, but their utterance IN CONTEXT—so it has to be a word or phrase that is familiar or expected in a familiar or expected context. It has to be bad at those two levels, not just a familiarity, but a familiarity inside a familiarity. Change one or the other and you have subverted or redeemed the cliché. A trite line from a love poem could be humorous, ironic, or scary if used in a poem on murder or politics or some minor trifle. The point is that clichés—even if they seem naked—are only *seeming* clichés if they are inverted or subverted or subsumed, and that is not a distinction without a difference!

Hence, *Grandma*, the poem, is a masterwork of decontextualizing what could be a banal poem, and furthermore, it's not just how it does that with the visual placement of words and lines, but that Bruce actually lets the reader know **in** the poem that he will do so when he writes, '*All of my thoughts trail off / From a loving memory.*' He then brilliantly shows what he has told, thereby utterly gutting that oldest of literary clichés: *show don't tell*. Well, my rejoinder to that is if you can tell as wonderfully or greatly as a Wallace Stevens, or Bruce in this poem, then FUCK that cliché!

But, before the next poem, let me use Hart Crane's great poem, *My Grandmother's Love Letters*, as a comparison against Bruce's trio of great poems in the same vein:

> There are no stars tonight
> But those of memory.
> Yet how much room for memory there is
> In the loose girdle of soft rain.
>
> There is even room enough
> For the letters of my mother's mother,
> Elizabeth,
> That have been pressed so long
> Into a corner of the roof
> That they are brown and soft,
> And liable to melt as snow.
>
> Over the greatness of such space
> Steps must be gentle.
> It is all hung by an invisible white hair.
> It trembles as birch limbs webbing the air.
>
> And I ask myself:
>
> 'Are your fingers long enough to play
> Old keys that are but echoes:
> Is the silence strong enough
> To carry back the music to its source
> And back to you again
> As though to her?'
>
> Yet I would lead my grandmother by the hand
> Through much of what she would not understand;
> And so I stumble. And the rain continues on the roof
> With such a sound of gently pitying laughter.

This is a great poem and tightly woven emotionally and in the symbolic hiding of his kin's love letters, we get a sense of time and imagination, as Crane approaches his past memories in assorted ways, and returns to where he started, the roof above it all, and the change in tone from fear of that past's possible destruction to the possible destroyer, the rain, almost mocking said past. This is certainly another masterful poem, but I want the reader to step back and evaluate Bruce's 3 poems against Crane's.

Crane was certainly possessed of a vocabulary well beyond Bruce's, as well as a technical ability to deploy those words. Where Bruce was simple, Crane was dense. But the mathematical metaphor and complexity of *Square World*, told in simpler language, is certainly every bit the equal of Crane's lingual capacity, and the density of the emotional listing in *Good Grief* is also equal to the intellectual density in Crane's poem. Finally, *Grandma*'s bravura plainspoken word choices, complexed upward by the placement of the lines, evokes a direct emotion in its breathiness, that is the equal or superior of Crane's poem because of the very simplicity of Bruce's word choices relative to Crane's word choices, yet towing a similar relative creative complexity.

Now, I am not denigrating *My Grandmother's Love Letters*, simply showing that while Crane's poem is justly famed for its writing as an emotional nod to his past, Bruce's 3 poems are its equal, at worst, and in *Grandma*, as a paean to his past, Bruce likely trumps Crane in overall depth and breadth of technical poetic virtuosity in his takes on his grandmother.

As mentioned, one of the overlooked and underappreciated aspects of poetic acumen, though, is the undermining or rehabilitation of clichés in any work of art, but most especially in poetry where the ill effects of banality are so easy to hone in on, and yet so difficult to do without simply and more easily just discarding the cliché. The next few poems of Bruce's that I will share are prime examples of redeeming clichés. The first poem I will tackle is one I tackled before in this essay called *Redeeming Clichés* (http://www.cosmoetica.com/S12-DES8.htm), and it is a great ario. So, let me just recapitulate what I wrote 20 years ago:

> Why'd You Do That?
>
> Grace walked down the sidewalk and swallowed
> My heart like a Nabisco cracker. It wasn't until
> Years later I was able to look up at what happened.
>
> My time had come. The day was done.
> Either get it or get out.
> Why don't you grow up?

But it put trouble <u>on the run</u>
And <u>bounce in my step</u> to think
<u>Everything was at stake</u>

And <u>nothing was lost</u>... <u>like a sunset</u>.

The 1ˢᵗ 8 underlined phrases would be definite clichés, while 'like a sunset' is clichéd in idea, more than phrasing. But let's go chronologically, see why the poem works so well, & why the 'apparent' clichés are not clichés- & throw a shrimp on the fuckin' barby for the Big Down   Under!

Title- a damned good 1. Note that 'That' is capitalized- this stresses that something VERY unusual has occurred. Also, the query is rhetorical, yet connects well with the last ½ of stanza 1- 'what happened' must be 'That'. What it is is a mystery- or is it? Does not the 1ˢᵗ ½ of the stanza answer that? Probably- but not definitely. But the title sets the whole drama of the poem- as well the tone- humorous, yet genuine.

On to stanza 1. Is Grace a female name, or an emotional demeanor? Either way, look how Grace has captured the speaker: 'swallowed/My heart like a Nabisco cracker'. How easily Bruce could have gone cliché. Instead, even the nonspecificity of the cracker type- save the brand name- serves to give a quirky feel to the poem. You wanna read on. It is the very oddity, yet simplicity, of stanza 1 which sets up the rest of the poem. This stanza's tone makes the seeming clichés that later appear just 'seeming' clichés. Also, stanza 1 has no clichés- seeming or real. & the sentence 'It wasn't until/Years later I was able to look up at what happened.' is the emotional ground for the whole poem. This stanza rocks, both in its wording & in the purpose it serves for the whole success of the poem. & look at line 1's end- is that a gasser, or what? Funny faux melodrama, in tune with the rest of the poem, yet the 1ˢᵗ word of the next line removes the humor & recontexts it into a serious mode. Talk about turning on an emotional dime!

Stanza 2 seems to have 4 clichés in 3 lines. Look again. They are NOT clichés because they buffet each other & the usual setups & outcomes that make the 4 seeming clichés clichés are not present. 'My time had come' has no fatalism attached to it, no resolute acceptance. 'The day was done' comes on its heels & seems a nonsequitur. That both phrases are full sentences & ½ of the line only emphasizes how unusual the line is. Unusuality is antithetical to triteness. It may not be good of itself, but triteness is not its weakness. The 2ⁿᵈ line that follows would be a cliché in some political poem, or a poem on a relationship- but not in a bizarre interior monologue which leads up to another rhetorical question/reproval: 'Why don't you grow up?' Yet, this line ties directly back to the question of the title. They almost bookend the incident they reference- that of Grace's capture of the speaker's heart.

But the poem does not stop there. Stanza 3 begins by subverting the 'on the run' cliché by making *trouble* the subject. At 1st blush this seems a nonsequitur too. But, we see it's perfectly in line with 'That', Grace's capture, & 'what happened'. We later realize trouble's run is companion to a bouncy step, which prelude the speaker's melodramatic statement that 'Everything was at stake'- presumably his/her heart.

That leads directly to the last stanza/line. The 'nothing was lost' comes right after, & contributes to, the melodrama of the preceding 2 stanzas, which played off the wonderful setup of the title & 1st stanza. We are on this wonderful rollercoaster that screeches to an ellipsis, which acts like a pregnant pause in a Borscht Belt comedian's routine: bada-boom. We then ease in to the familiar scene of a sunset ending (serenity). Yet, coming here it is totally unexpected. & what would seem like a cheesy attempt at emotion rings genuine, because it is not lost, sunsets happen every day. This ties back to the end of stanza 1, which tied back to the title. We get this hidden continuity in the poem's seeming jaggered tale. This poem succeeds so well because of its dramatic cadence, the odd order of events, their seemingly banal recitation, & devastating timing. The emotional depth is heightened precisely because the poem's quirky, humorous feel lowers the reader's emotional guard.

Now, compare this to many a bad poem that will have clichés littered across it. Those poems will fail because they lack the redeeming qualities aforementioned: cadence, order, & timing. Stanza 1 is long-lined & contemplative. Then the poem's images are punctuated by periods or line breaks. The seeming clichés are thrown so quickly at you that they blur, until the ellipsis.... then exhalation. This is a marvelously constructed poem. Its music is not so much in the use of rime, assonance, or alliteration, but in its delicate & intricate construction. How many poems, laden with clichés, are leaden in music? Either they overcompensate & force alliteration, or they are bits of chopped up prose.

But this was not the only time Bruce indulged in and inverted cliché, and did so likely with no clue to what nor why nor how he was doing it.

This next poem is a publishable ario:

Perspective

Life is perspective and vice versa
Like leverages against a daunting reality
A view from the mountain top.

Most anything can be processed
And broken like a football field
Or music into notes.

It's the hardest to see yourself -
A creation or creator?
Half full or half empty?

Walk in my shoes and you tell me.

How many clichés can you spot? And how does Bruce redeem the poem from being a total cliché, in and of itself? And how does it not succeed as well as the prior poem, *Why'd You Do That?* Is it that the first poem had a better opening stanza? Or maybe this poem has a less interesting title, among other things?

Let me move on to another poem—a publishable ario—that succeeds, if not greatly, in being a good poem, by subverting clichés:

Hampered

I must have had my hands tied behind my back
Been blindfolded and standing on one leg
To not see it coming.

How did I think I could get away with it
Or pull the wool over everyone's eyes
And still walk in the light.

I had heard you must pay the piper
I just never thought there'd be so many musicians
Who went well beyond confessions

And got into heavy judgments.

Again, a poem with over half a dozen clichés that would seem wholly naked if not for the air of mystery Bruce clothes the whole poem in, starting with its ambiguous one-word title. The poem basically revolves around the meaning of the word 'it,' which in its double appearance seems initially to be a part of two separate clichés but soon turns out to be a much more philosophically deep thing, which is emphasized by the last 3 lines which seem to screw the poem in another direction than what we first are presented with. This cannot wrench the poem up to greatness, but it makes this ario a worthwhile curio that bears multiple readings and can possibly mean different things to different people.

This next poem—also a publishable ario—is not as layered in clichés throughout, as the previous poems, but it does weight its seeming clichés into the last 4 lines:

It's Lent

Ash Wednesday tonight like a door
Swung open and a challenge
To wrestle with myself

With the purpose of goodness
Coming through insight
And thoughts now I don't know.

But I do know that something is out there
Calling me
I must put one foot out then the other

Until I meet a destiny I never will.

So, how does this poem handle its seeming clichés? First, it opens with an odd but intriguing 6-line premise that hints at a negation of something that is sort of riffed on in the last 4 lines, and especially the final line wherein we get not only a negation but a seeming logical absurdity: 'Until I meet a destiny I never will.' Unless it is something other and means that the speaker will meet a destiny he will not call forth into existence by volition. Hence, the speaker has given himself over to fate. And note how line 6 seems to augur line 10's different meanings of *will*.

Of course, there is more in this and all the poems tackled than what I sketch here, but this aids my argument that Bruce was a poet whose simplicity of poetic construction was not always what it seemed to be. Under the placid surface of seeming clichés the work was often Negatively Capable and stippled with assorted derangements.

This is very true in this next great ario we will examine:

I'll Whisper It

Can you handle it if I just whisper it?
I won't come in with the guns blazing
Just warm intentions, smiling.

Have a rendezvous but in the light

Under the shadow of a tree
Out in the midst of the woods

Just as day breaks we will embrace
As though we can't get enough
Of each other's unspent attention.

Then, then... then.

Ok. Let us examine why this poem works. Perhaps it gets back to the concept of *it* that hangs over the poem, as it did not too many poems ago? It seems clear that the *it* referenced here is love, and that the couple mentioned may want to say they love the other person. Hence, the clichés that follow are an attempt to soft pedal a declaration that can change lives. After the clichés the poem twists on a dime and we find out two things in the final two lines—that the couple cannot get enough of each other's attentions, even though it is 'unspent,' which harkens directly back to *It's Lent*'s meeting of a destiny that will possibly never be. Yet this poem pushes such a cognitive dissonance even further, in that it almost seems, in the last line, that we have been here before, watching this couple, and their emotional impotence before, and will again in the near future. And, make no mistake that there is impotence here, as the 3rd stanza clearly delineates that the couple's embrace is not an acceptance of the love they have difficulty even whispering, but a possible parting. Go ahead, reread that ending. Is the not getting enough of each other's unspent attention a post-love and/or sex scenario, or is it a saying goodbye that forces a parting embrace? And do all the clichés act as a balm for the coming departure? And what of the tripled ending of the last line, and the two different punctuation marks?

Now I want to examine two different ways Bruce handles wintry themes, in a great ario titled *Living the Snowfall*, and a publishable ario titled *Snowy Impressions*:

Living The Snowfall

The snow drifts like a sonnet from the sky
In small flakes of neon.

It lights up the coldness and makes me smile.

In pockets on the ground blown together
It makes a blanket across the city
Covering the barren gray ground.

I wonder where it all came from -
(I mean besides the clouds).
A sparkling form

Too real to disregard or misunderstand.

Snowy Impressions

The sky looks distant but clear
Thin ice that goes deeply above me
So I plant my feet and wait.

Coming down several hours
A day later and more like night
Except for the whiteness of my musings.

Light. Very light.
A feather would be heavier.
Men and women shoveling

Dust of a winter's landing.

Both are poems worth reading, but the first has a better music—with alliteration, as well as better metaphors, although mid-poem it returns to what seems to be a cliché (*snow as blanket*) but its descriptions before and after that moment show why that seeming descent into banality is not damning but grounding to the poem. First, look at the title, as it can be read as the speaker being a part of the snow, a sort of cognitive storm musing on its own existence, save that that which it sees—its cousins, if you will—are different, even if part of the same storm. Then the actual poem starts with the snow's drift like a sonnet—an intellectual thing, further emboldening the idea that the snowstorm is sentient, and it ends with the snow wondering where it, or itself, came from, and the final line is just a killer twist as the living snow reasserts its reality. Now, could this great poem have been even greater with the change of that middle's snow blanket and barren ground? Yes, but *great* poems are not *perfect* poems. Some can be, but they are usually two distinct things, and great trumps perfect, for perfect usually means technical and/or musical perfection over a depth of insight and excellent phrasing. The best example of poems that are perfect but not great can be seen in those written by English poet Walter de la Mare (1873 – 1956), whose verse is a boon to the ear, but a slop on the mind. And a great poem does not mean cliché-free—and by that I mean not just seeming clichés but actual naked clichés—for a single lapse does not necessarily sink a poem's greatness, although it does remove said poem from any claim on perfection. Just look at some of Shakespeare's great sonnets to see loads of clichés that don't damn the poem, or his whole play, like *Romeo And Juliet* or *King Lear*— considered a classic by many critics, even while trite in its writing.

I have written perfect poems and I have written great poems, and sometimes the two qualities are in a single poem, and other times not, as I stated. Given a choice between mere perfection and greatness, I, and any sane artist, will always choose greatness, because perfection can be lifeless and hermetic, while greatness is often not, although, as I mentioned earlier, near great works of art are usually the best works for study of how an artwork and an artist works because the minor flaws of a near great work often allow the *in* to how the work and its artist accomplish the greatness they do in that bear great and other great works, which, like perfect works, can often seem functionally and intellectually hermetic.

The second poem is a good to very good poem, but not even near great. It does not intellectually take on a new view of a snowstorm, it just uses mostly familiar imagery with a couple of interesting moments—such as the sky being thought of as thin ice the speaker sees from below, as well as its ending, wherein the shoveled snow is not just a dust of snow but winter itself having landed. This poem's inversions are not as strong and unexpected as *Living The Snowfall*'s, but then the title itself, *Snowy Impressions*, is a bit mitigating, even if not wholly for the poem is just impressions—fleet musings of a moment, and not the embodiment of a force of nature. The first poem takes on the mantle of greatness, anchors it in the middle, and then nails the poem at the end. The second poem's veer into banal imagery does not soar to the heights the first poem does. That is the difference, qualitatively, in these two similar works. The former poems inverts expectations very well, while the second is a good, solid take with a novel moment or two.

Let me use this publishable non-ario as an example to explain what good enjambment can do. Enjambment is how a poet breaks his poem into lines.

The Cut

My father cut himself
And I flinched.
He looked down at his hand
As if the blood was foreign to his body.
The cut wasn't bad
But it still chilled me
The way he reacted
Or did not react to pain.
I learned that toughness
Can be almost inhuman.
Sweat almost came off my brow
At seeing this.
I was flabbergasted
I didn't realize to feel was criminal.

Let's look at the last 2 lines of this good poem. The bulk of the poem is lineated into discrete statements of a memory in the speaker's past, yet something odd occurs at the poem's end. Lines 13 and 14 can be read as discrete statements—the speaker stating that he was put off by the situation and then thinking that his emotions might be seen as weak to his tougher father. But, given that there are periods scattered in the rest of the poem, that these two lines are not two distinct sentences, which they could be, the last two lines can be read as one whole sentence, which then inverts what I just stated about them as two separate sentences. In this case, the speaker is astonished at his lack of realization regarding emotion—quite a different take than in the two sentences mode it can be read as. Still, this is hardly the only example of Bruce's that makes use of enjambment, but its coming at poem's end, and the rather straightforward difference a mere period makes is what allows this to be a useful example.

On to another publishable ario:

Sin

In the sacred walls within my church
Within my heart
I'm able to watch my sin fly.

A holy setting, an ideal place
For me
To let them go.

I can raise my eyes
To the stainglass windows
And see

Like a sheep his home in the hay.

Note how line 2 can be read as either a further delineation of line 1, or the entree into line 3, or as the connector between lines 1 and 3. Are the sacred walls of the speaker's church literally within his heart? This is where a lack of punctuation can confuse or conflate, and the difference in perception is not a choice between good and bad, just a choice each reader can make in the act of co-creation with the artist.

But let me return to clichés and poems that are parts of *de facto* series or variations on a theme. Bruce has three poems in this collection, written years apart, dealing with fences, and they form a *de facto* trilogy.

Let me use this publishable ario, dealing with *the grass is always greener* cliché as an example:

Over The Fence

So much is permanent like a fence
I considered it a lost cause
Thought I would be peering over jealously forever.

But that's all in the past now.
Climbed night and day
To get over the fence

Just to get to the pasture
Where the grass is greener – exponentially,
By a margin of 1 to 50.

Will take time just to adjust a bit.

Let me state, Bruce is at his best when he plays with clichés—even if not consciously knowing he is doing so—rather than indulging them. Subversions, inversions, redemptions, twists of clichés are all better. Now, the poem does not subvert all its clichés, like 'I considered it a lost cause' nor 'that's all in the past now,' but the one time he overwhelms the cliché is in line 9. Go ahead, read the poem, and get to that line. See it?

No?

Ok, in line 8, Bruce writes 'Where the grass is greener – exponentially,' yet line 9 says 'By a margin of 1 to 50,' which is the opposite of exponentiality. He should have written '50 to 1', meaning the grass over the fence is 50 times better, not 1/50th. And I am certain this was a total error on Bruce's part, and had we seen this at the UPG it would have been universally pointed out as an error. Yet, the last line, 'Will take time just to adjust a bit' is meant for the 50 to 1 idea, meaning the speaker has to adjust to the bounty, when in reality the greenness, or good of the other side is 1/50th the expectation, therefore the speaker will have to adjust to less.

Here is a perfect example where a line or image or metaphor in poetry that is verging on trite, in its intended form, becomes something transformative in its mistaken deviation from the expected. It's not enough to lift the poem into greatness, but it ensures the poem is a worthwhile poem in Bruce's canon.

I earlier did a side-by-side comparison of two thematically similar poems, and will now do the same for several poems of Bruce's wherein there were two versions of the same poem that were different, yet there was no obviously later nor superior version of the poem. The only differences were the inclusion of exclusion of certain lines, words, metaphors, punctuation, etc. Read them both, think them over, and see if you prefer one or the other, and then ask yourself why?

First are two versions of a publishable non-ario:

Serious At Life (1)

I blink at life
To see more clearly
Where and what it is.

I once stared straight
Into hell.
I now walk beside life.
Sometimes I gather my storm
And I go to the rooftops
Or higher.
Mostly, I think.
I play cautious ball
And I intertwine routine.

Serious At Life (2)

I blink at life
To see clearly
Where and what it is.
I once stared straight
Into the face of death,
I now walk beside life.
Sometimes I gather my storm
And I go to rooftops
Or higher.
Mostly, I think
I play cautious ball
And I intertwine routine.

A solid poem, either way, and the only difference is in the line 5's: 'Into hell,' vs. 'Into the face of death.' The change slightly changes the meaning of the poem, yet both versions are utter clichés, so does it matter? I'd take Version (1) simply because its cliché is shorter.
Another publishable non-ario this time:

Viewing the Pine (1)

The pine tree in my neighbor's yard
Towers over the blue roof.
It goes much higher than
My mild hopes for human welfare tonight.
Strong branches build up
To heights that are simply beyond my reach.
I give the tree my today
Because it existed yesterday.
Farther along I see myself growing
Tall and strong like the pine.
I see humanity grasping the height

Surpassing its measure now.
I see the pine bowing lowly
To the onward growth of humankind
Finally I see the pine and me as one –
A combination of what is and what is to become.

Viewing the Pine (2)

The pine tree in my neighbor's yard
Towers over the blue roof.
It goes much higher than
My mild hopes for human welfare tonight.
Strong branches build up
To heights that are simply beyond my reach.
I give the tree my today
Because it existed yesterday.
Farther along I see myself growing
Tall and strong like the pine.
I see humanity grasping the height

This pair sees the second version dropping the last 4 lines of the poem. It's a shorter, tighter poem, and its end without a period leaves the poem literally open-ended on a posit. The first version, however, is longer and not open-ended, and it encompasses all the second version does and adds a philosophical depth the second lacks, but are the extra, sometimes obvious claims worth it? I say they are about of equal worth, hence I would not have included both in the book, whereas many a poem had lesser and better versions.

On to another publishable non-ario—and it's worth noting that none of the alternate versions of these poems ever reached the heights of greatness, as most were lateral or sideways changes.

I Stumbled (1)

Stumbling no not falling
I only stumbled a little
Tripped up by problems
But I didn't fall
No, I remember I slipped
But I don't think anybody noticed
A small light downward movement
But not a complete fallout.

I Stumbled (2)

Stumbling, no not falling
I only stumbled a little
Tripped up by problems
But I didn't fall.
No, I remember I slipped
But I don't think anybody noticed,
A small light downward movement
But not a complete fallout.

These poems are virtually identical, save for some minor punctual changes. See them? How does mere punctuation change a poem or a line?

Here is a publishable ario, with the first one possibly the later version:

Indications (1)

The highway crew spins yarn from their coffee as I
Pass down the vein back into Minneapolis.
Road construction riveted into my being like sound.

There will be a better road to travel - to get to know
Eventually. As it grows perpendicular to this city
There is a hint of growth suppressed only by material limits.

I'm really ageless the changes going on around me
Don't stop or settle because that's all there is.
And I don't mind really even though I can't keep up

I try with one more line... one more eyeful... another taste of it.

Indications (2)

The highway crew spins yarn from their coffee as I
Pass down the vein back into Minneapolis.
Road construction riveted into my being like sound.

There will be a better road to travel - to get to know
Eventually. As it grows perpendicular to this city
There is a hint of growth suppressed only by material limits.

I'm really ageless, the changes going on around me
Don't stop or settle because that's all there is.
And I don't mind really even though I can't keep up

I try with one more line... one more eyeful... another taste of it.

What are the differences here? A comma in line 7 and an italicized word in line 10—the only italicized word in the whole book, I believe. How do these minor changes affect the poem?

Now a publishable non-ario:

Waiting For A Bus (1)

Open eyes
And staring

Sunshine hot

Compensation
For the waiting

Is cool air
In the bus

When will it come?
Now? Later?
Today? Tomorrow?

I wait.
It's not so bad.

Sunshine hot
Gosh it's hot.

When the bus comes
There will be
Cool air.

I wait.

Waiting For The Bus (2)

Open eyes
And staring
Sunshine hot

Compensation
For waiting
Is cool air
In the bus

When will it come?
Now? Later?
Today? Tomorrow?

I wait.

It's not so bad.

Sunshine hot
Gosh it's hot.

When the bus comes
There will be cool air.

I wait.

Here the changes are in the title and the enjambment, which influences the stanza construction. What effect do these have?

The next publishable non-ario is a combination of 2 versions of the poem—one in a later WORD document, and the other in an earlier typed-out paper version. This is a poem that I seem to recall Bruce bringing to the UPG, but the Word version seems to be post-UPG, and he seems to have embodied many of my dicta for enjambment here. Still, both versions of this poem had merit so I took the best from both, and all the lines that resulted are fully Bruce lines. I do not *Schneiderize* others' poems, even when I think they are making poor choices:

Bus Window

Every ray I see through
The mud stained window
Is like fresh air.

The bus window, splashed
By some errant vehicle,
Has left me almost blind.

My stop comes.
I disembark.
Now I'm out there where
I couldn't see before.
The buildings: skyscrapers
Which are so tall
Are worth more than a life
To them.

It wasn't always that way.
The world's bigger than
I can manage.
I want to retreat
To my bus window.
Vision, now open,
Drinks intoxicating sights
Today. I'm not seeing
Rightly. Still the muddy
Window hangs before my eyes.

Aside from having two slightly different versions of the same poem in the book, Bruce also has a pair of paired publishable arios that are wholly different poems, yet have the same title:

Rejection (1)

There's only one rejection that's permanent
And I don't believe that is either.
Don't lose course or hang your head

Time will heal that wound
And there'll be a ship on the horizon
God will let out some line, then pull you in.

Pay no matter that what people saw in you
Has been rejected
If it was worthwhile, it's still there.

Just never, ever reject yourself.

Rejection (2)

Rejection causes immediate grief
Because you wanted something
You couldn't have.

Your apple cart is toppled
Your dime misspent
Your one chance vanished

Before you nothing
It's all behind now
Just can't quite realize it

You must just take steps now.

This next pair of publishable arios does not even need parenthesized numerals after them, as the different poems are separated by one having a question mark in its title.

Standards

I like people with standards
At one time it almost didn't matter what they were.
But now it does.

It's got to be standards that work for the good
Standards that say, 'Look what I've achieved.'
'I set a goal and accomplished it.'

Not so much, 'I've never done this or that.'
Where's the life to that?
You can't rest your laurels on what you haven't done.

Being able to forgive sins ranks high.

Standards?

Having standards won't help grief
Kings and queens suffer grief
It can affect one and all.

Certain measures can be taken
Stay active, journal, eat chocolate
Have a routine, sleep, eat healthy

But you can't work it out
Think it through
Or get over it.

You must make friends and bear it.

So, now that we have dug into some of the technical side of
Bruce's poems, it is time to speak more of the man behind the
poetry—not the *poet*, per se, but the man himself.

I earlier mentioned Bruce's fetish for women's nylons, and while
known to me, Jess, and a few other UPGers. Bruce did not often talk
of it, and when he did so there was a mix of shame and joy in his
demeanor. I would not have even mentioned this aspect of his life
had not Bruce explicitly written a publishable ario on the subject:

Her Nylons

I've always liked the look of nylons
On women as they wisked down the sidewalk
Showing off their most beautiful legs.

I could almost be a crossdresser
Wearing nylons at home
To feel their silkiness next to my skin.

But I believe I will find a woman someday
Who greets me at the door at night

Wearing nothing but sheer stockings

And an invitation to touch.

This poem is clearly a fantasy, but Bruce's claim that he could *almost* be a crossdresser is true. But, as far as I know he was not, he only would wear the nylons at home and briefly looking into a mirror, so he was hardly a transvestite, but I did mention that when Bruce was into drugs and at his worst mental state he did pay for sex with prostitutes—and that was likely the only sex he ever had in his life, as I mentioned his earlier poetic declaration of going 30+ years in his later life without sex.

This next publishable ario is not explicit in the choice to be made, but Bruce did tell me the biggest choice he made in his life was to reform—leave the drugs, alcohol and prostitutes behind. For better or worse, Bruce chose his God:

The Choice You Make

Stairs leading to the second floor
The third and so forth to the top
Where you are greeted by Deity

The challenge starts.
Glass doors, errant kites, and backrubs
Walking, skipping, limping

Is it the past? Can't be the future.
Must be the present
Where you get a grip

Never ever saying never.

Of course, this choice led Bruce to concomitant and subsequent beliefs, choices, and lifestyles. In light of the 2022 U.S. Supreme Court's overturning of a woman's right to an abortion, Bruce's rare politicality in these next two publishable arios is surprising, even shocking, for him:

Why Can't You Control Your Motorcycles?

I want freedom too,
But when did freedom become

Six men raping one woman?

You thought you were driving your bikes in the sun.
Instead you drove your motorcycles straight between her legs.
I want to see the look on her face.

Why couldn't you control your motorcycles?
You went too far beyond the bend.
You sailed right into moonrock in the Vatican.

Now she will park your bikes.

What is the metaphor here? The ending seems almost like an *anti-ario*. Strange but it grips one at the start.
Here is another:

She's Got A Right To Say, 'No'

People have a right to draw a line
In the sand like my preacher
Said he'd do about abortion.

He was all about pro-choice
And women need rights
To include saying, 'No'.

They are not required to say, 'Yes'
To any wild question from the stratosphere.
Sometimes 'No' works.

And they don't need me to tell them that.

It was rare for Bruce to be so straight forward in verse, or life, yet this poem is not modern virtue signaling, simply truly righteous and justified indignation and anger, as the last line basically is Bruce knowing his place in such a controversy.

But, of all the things I have spoken of re: Bruce's life, verse, themes, obsessions, repeated claims, none really come close to his love for Minneapolis. That's why this book is titled *THE Minneapolis Poet*!

Here is a great ario that is also a pre-UPG poem that embodies my claim:

The Parameters Of Downtown Minneapolis

The breadth of downtown Minneapolis
Can be seen in the breadth of countless red taillights
Leaving on one way streets going out

To suburbs and other hidden places
While downtown lingers in my mind
And upon my feet that know I'm not leaving.

The height of downtown Minneapolis
Is witnessed in buildings
Etching their designs upon my opened face.

And the depth is seen by perceiving eyes.

Note how the three physical dimensions each get shorter yet sharper delineations, yet the last line is not openly stated to be experienced by the speaker of the poem, presumably Bruce. Likely without knowing it, Bruce displaced the poem's grounding from the speaker perceiving Minneapolis to an unknown percipient's look at either Minneapolis or the speaker's 'opened face.'

The next 3 poems deal with Twin Cities-specific events, such as the annual end of year holiday season Holidazzle Parade in Minneapolis, in this publishable ario:

A Smiley Parade

The 'Holi-Dazzle' parade carries its weight
In a spectacular light show
To carry us through the winter solstice.

You can't help but grin at the prospect of a parade in December
Offering fairy tale characters bedecked in light bulbs
Dancing down the main street in town.

This night's special guests, The Rockettes,
Were placed on a float
While lesser dancers roamed freely.

It was all over after Santa Claus gloated on by.

The last line contains what is probably a typo—the word *gloated* for *floated*, as *g* and *f* are next to each other on the Qwerty keyboard,

68

yet I was unable to find another take on the poem that contained the word *floated,* so instead of *correcting* the seeming error, I left it as *gloated.* It seems a more active word, plus it somehow makes Santa somewhat sinister, and somehow above God, in that Santa's commercialism has triumphed.

The next publishable ario deals with the summer equivalent of the Holidazzle Parade, and that is the local Torchlight Parade, in which free events and good are part of a multi-day festival.

Torchlighter

Shifts of participants steady
And we, the rest, rest before
The sun goes down.

We are rails of a track
Octopi displaced
The coming of a train

And we are not disappointed
Night flow of entertainment
Different marchers

In the ongoing...

Bruce also has a number of poems that reference Minneapolis geography, such as this publishable non-ario:

Lake Street

Cars roll along Lake Street
And a pink building says it all.
Young toughs in their cars -
Poor cars - not of the wealthy type.

They look for life and meaning
Along this narrow avenue

When the cosmos is so vast -
So like a young mind on Lake Street.

But, at his center, Bruce was about more than whatever the subject of his poem was. Poetry, even more so than religion, was at the core of Bruce's existence, yet he could write terrible poems in long barren swathes of energy, then hit on a great poem. And his skill set was often erratic. Look at this publishable ario that is an otherwise good poem, even as its word choices and punctuation do not take advantage of the named musicality its title could lend its construction, and then utterly tanks in its last line:

Waltz In Waltz Out

Sometimes you hardly know you've been there
Except you've got a receipt
And there's a chunk of your watch gone.

But down the road you remember
Could be the fragrance that gives it away
And you wonder if it matters.

There are no pictures, no tape recordings
You're sure no one will know
But you know better

The long hard night has just begun.

But Bruce could not only damage a poem at its end; he could make it stumble out of the gate, as in this publishable ario:

Ice

Ice. The kind that makes you feel like a popsicle.
All over the streets. Manhandling the sidewalks.
Bitter. Cold.

The bus is way late
And I'm freezing
A hockey player out of the game.

I feel like a gerbil being tested in a lab
To see how much I can take
Or if I'll just solidify.

Reset. Somewhere a river flows and a bird sings.

It is usually a waste of verbiage to repeat a word or line as the opening of a poem, when that word or line is the title. This poem would be way better had Bruce had a different title, or just started with 'The kind that makes you....' The only argument *for* the poem's start as it is is as a counterpoint to the last line's single word opening then period, but even that could be bettered with a single word like 'Set.' to open the poem, and anticipate the last line's first word and cast the poem into a circular pattern.

In the next publishable ario Bruce coins a word:

> Don't Stop There
>
> It's only a plateau of another mountain
> Which is only half
> The distance of a true stretch.
>
> I usually play for the middle
> But that's with economics
> And class structure and that kind of thing.
>
> When I'm on a journey I like to go the whole way
> Spiveling especially towards the sun
> Except when it gets too hot
>
> And something must be done.

What in the hell does 'spiveling' mean? It cannot be 'swiveling' as *p* and *w* are well separated on a Qwerty keyboard, yet even that word makes little sense in the poem's context. A hermetic little ario mystery, indeed. Yet, one can imagine someone like Bruce spiveling to the sun, especially so!

The next publishable ario deals with Bruce's acquaintances abandoning him during his low years of the early 1980s, and opens with some odd imagery (salt, jewels) that could be sexual:

> Am I Salty Yet?
>
> Once upon a time I lost my salt
> And I felt my jewels of wisdom
> Being trampled underfoot.
>
> I'm not going to say what led up to this
> Suffice it to say it was complex
> And people were unable to help when they tried.

The hardest part was the hate
I felt from those who misunderstood me
And relegated me to their delete file.

Saw a lot of behinds then.

Are the behinds referenced asses or buttocks or just people turning
their backs to him?

This next publishable ario misses greatness by its opacity, yet we
still get a sense of the speaker's being an outsider:

Going Now

Beyond the stick, past the ball,
Through the book, above the lamp
Over the PC, on top of the window.

With my feet I will walk.
Transformations sifting reality
Thunderstruck.

I'm alone always alone
Conquering, conquesting yesterdays
Until the uprising

Is little more than a haughty glance.

This next publishable non-ario is one of a number of poems from
the 1980s or early 1990s that I would term a *proto-ario*—that is a
poem that has elements of the classic ario, but is not there yet—
either it's 10 lines but not in the 3-3-3-1 format, or it has too many
stanzas or lines. In this poem one can sense Bruce coming close to
but not realizing the power of a single set-apart last line:

Spring

Fall winds blew once sending
Chills along my spine
Telling us that winter was coming.

Winter winds blew cold snow
And the harshness caused me
To go inward and tighten.

I waited for signs of Spring.

Spring came and blew warm winds
That set my spirit soaring so high.

I live in Spring now,
Etching out the limits of life.

This next publishable non-ario is also a proto-ario wherein the last line is set apart but the rest of the poem is longer than 9 lines in 3-line stanzas. It also deals with Bruce's many blue-collar jobs, a trait he infused in his verse and prose as I did in mine, even though our lives and jobs were often quite different:

It's A Job

Today I hold a dustrag;
Yesterday it was a vacuum and a buffer.
It's my job.

Like an old bathroom towel
That's been used beyond its freshness,
I work on.

As if I'm a trampoline however
I bounce that idea straight away
Because I know the importance of working.

I work as though I'm conducting
A symphony to God.

My dustrag glides over furniture.
My vacuum whisks over the floor,
And my buffer sings over the tile.

Somewhere along the line I forgot I was working.

This poem could be considered a *long poem* by Bruce, as in all of his poetry, in this book or not, I cannot recall a single non-ario poem that exceeded a typed page in length.

Let us return to a typical publishable ario dealing with Bruce's work as a janitor in the 1980s:

Dust Had Settled

Dust had settled on the office furniture,
Various electronic equipment,
And books.

It's not from non-use but high-use,
And it was a quiet moment in the morning
When I took out the wand.

Doing a quick flick with my hand
Dust particles were banished to the air
Sent on the run

Probably to resettle some other time.

First, the past tense title is NOT a cliché. Why? Because, as I stated earlier a cliché is an expected or familiar element in its expected or familiar context. Dash that formula and you have subverted the banality. Bruce is writing of *literal* dust here, not metaphoric dust, as he executes his janitorial duties.

Back to the ario form, or not. This publishable non-ario is NOT an ario as its only written form, while 10 lines, does not adhere to the 3-3-3-1 lineal format.

Symphony Concert

The sweet music flows from
Structured hands

To an appreciative audience.

Sounds somewhere between
Melancholy and sunshine
Hover over dark suited musicians.

I listen with great concentration
Paying my respects
To the civilized manners
That lift me to dignity.

Imagine this poem formatted as an ario, and does that, alone, improve it?

Here is a publishable non-ario that again deals with dust and Bruce's janitorial duties:

Sometime Job

Rolling out the trash, vacuuming the dust
I'm on my route
Of my sorta job.

I don't mind sweating at a job
I do so I can write.

I nudge my mind into a daydream
And I'm high into the clouds
Cut loose and fancy-free

Doing my wheeling-dealing job.

In this publishable non-ario Bruce's title, *Week Ending*, could just as accurately been *Weak Ending*. I told Bruce at the UPG that he needed to drop the unneeded Melvillean last line, and had he this interesting poem with wordplay would have been better; but Bruce seems to have never even tried to improve this poem:

Week Ending

Lone day yields something
Blending the rest, blurring
All that grew together,
Dissipates like rain on the ground.
It surges and sways,
Kneeknocks me into a song
About relaxing and it
Soothes hinter undergirded
Powers to clouds above
Beyond and higher.
Rays through, together
Dropping me as I take time.
The birds are sparrows
The canteen gurgles
Past the river to the city
Of one people, underscores
My gravity.
No wrinkle, nothing gained.
Or lost.

It rolls off my watch
Into the ocean of the past.

And what an odd word choice *hinter* is here. Bruce may have not known the true meaning of the word is *behind*, and meant something else by its use.

In the below publishable non-ario we get an even more bold playfulness from Bruce; not only in the many ways three is referenced, but in the rare use of an ampersand which even resembles the numeral 3. The best line in the poem is line 10 which both flows with the narrative of the poem yet also establishes that 3 is the number of things of import:

Three

Important insignificant meaningful
Three periods, three innings
Three Gods in one.
The numeral 3
Bulges on the line
Like a stubborn trinity
Tricycles, triathlons, trilogies
Three-ring circuses, triplexes
and triple-feature Movies,
A number of important things -
Associated with the number three
Gives me time to think & 3 minutes to fry an egg.

Bruce's playfulness is also seen in the below publishable non-ario that is very unlike most of the rest of Bruce's corpus, and reminds of a great ario we saw earlier, *I'll Whisper It*:

Beat... Beat, Beat

Beat
The cry I hear
Of the city street.

Beat, beat
I'm down
At my brother's feet.

Beat, beat, beat
I'm homeless

And waging a war against...

Beat, beat,
...a life gone berserk
And grim.

Beat
My heart bounces down
The city street.

Beat, beat
No one to lay
Comfort...

Beat, beat, beat
...to eyes
swelled with...

Beat... beat, beat
...chaotic, formless,
Turmoil

Beat... Beat
day in and out.

Beat.

I should not make it seem as if Bruce was not poetically adventurous, even if he was best in a familiar form—the ario, whose growing frequency as poetic form of choice seemed to increase with the years. Yes, the ario dominates his poetry, but the little excursions into non-arios, as shown, had some successes, and it's not as if Bruce was alone in a more conservative approach to his craft. Most poets are. Rare is the poet that lets the form find its function, *or is that the other way around?*, I hear Bruce's voice asking me.

Let's gander at this great non-ario that leaves the reader in an M.C. Escherian world:

Urban Walkways

Sidewalks may catch my stride
In a jog or just a stroll
Any day of the week
As the time bides.

Weather permitting or not
I take my cause to their paths
Perhaps with no permission
Other than the life I've got.

Point A to point B -
That's sidewalk 1 to sidewalk 2
Perpendiculars
Then across on 3.

Asphalt, cement, new and old
Our sidewalks come in differing shape,
Form. Narrow notebooks of our feet,
Or strands or veins of the fold.

Note how the word 'form,' at line 15's start is a noun if read grammatically and syntactically as the last word of its sentence, but lineally as the first word and verb of line 15. Bruce occasionally did toss in a little razzle dazzle, even if it was his subconscious doing so.

Onto this great non-ario, a haiku—the only one Bruce seems to have written or maybe saved:

Envious Feelings

Oriental Green
So I gave it some sunlight
To watch it grow out.

As this is Bruce's lone foray and it succeeds so well in a classical *and* Bruce sense, well....

This next great non-ario is so odd, with phrasings that recall Bruce's women's nylons fetish, yet is so rich in typically clueless Bruce humor that the question at poem's end seems actually logical to the speaker. That Bruce could craft such a funny and almost extended William Carlos Williams (1883 – 1963) or e.e. cummings (1894 – 1962) like poem, again, well, what more can be said?

Running Away With Clothes

I've always liked the luster of clothes
Hiding our nakedness
And so much more.

Or do they enhance
Our walk from the Garden of Eden
Spread out in trousers or skirts?

Adam and Eve wore figs
And I - a pair of jeans
Which shows me something

About my nature
And men's and women's
And confusion over the two

Like me experimenting
And stopping just short
Of cowboy boots

With styles so diverse
Yet hiding me
Like a cloak in the closet

Even though since my youth
It was the most natural
Way to go:

To attire myself.
I won't spend a lot of money
Or time...

Clothes... Where did they come from?

The ending also begs the question of whether the speaker is naked
or not as he is soliloquizing. Given it is Bruce's poem, this is not a
rhetorical question.

Bruce Ario vs. Other Poets

Since I mentioned good old Dr. Williams above, I think it is time
to up my case and claims for Bruce Ario being a great poet. Period.
So now I will not just extol his poems' best qualities, but I will
compare his oeuvre to the works of well known and published poets
from yore up until the modern PC Elitists that dominate the MFA
Mafias of the modern 21st Century Big Publishing industry.

Let me start by comparing Bruce to poets whom most would think of as occupying some of the same areas of verse and thought that Bruce does—that of the weird. Recall, earlier, I wrote this:

> And Bruce did thrive in the arts by becoming something else I neglected to mention in this essay's opening. He became a weirdo. Well, specifically a *weirdo poet*, and in a bit I shall explain that and compare him with other notable weirdo artists and poets.

Let us get into it, but first by establishing what it means to be weird in an artistic sense. To the average person—be they online game player or amateur pornography enthusiast—calling an artist *weird* is, itself, an utter redundancy, for so few human beings can even make bad art, and not that many more even appreciate art of any merit.

When I speak of weirdo artists, though, I mean one of five things re: what the artist is/was....

> 1) weird in how they create(d) their art
> 2) creating/created weird art
> 3) likely very little known or wholly unknown, deservedly or not, in their lifetime
> 4) living/lived bizarrely in the pursuit of their art
> 5) all or a combination of the above points

Now, onto some well-known weirdo, or as some call them— *outsider* artists. I prefer *weirdo* because it is more specific. I and my wife, Jessica, are outsider artists due to the failures of the artistic infrastructure in America....but we are not weird. Well, we innovate and excel, so, yes, one may argue that those two qualities are, in a sense, weird or odd, but that's stretching it, especially in comparison to Bruce and truer weirdo artists like Vivian Maier (1926 – 2009) and Henry Darger (1892 – 1973), who are probably the two most spectacularly famed outsider and/or weirdo artists of the last few decades. Both lived in obscurity, modesty, and in Darger's case, poverty, and both only rocketed to fame posthumously, when another person discovered their art. Both have had major documentaries made of them, and both have seen their works enrich the bank accounts of people they never met, long after pelf could help either.

Of course, there is a huge difference between Maier and Darger, and that is that Maier is justly hailed as one of the great American photographers in history. Her photographs capture mid-20th Century America like few others have. She has been labeled a street photographer, but that really short shrifts her. Her personal life seemed to be one of artistic and romantic rejection, but an unending optimism in doing the work itself in a sort of ultimate art for art's sake devotion. And while her artistic work was great, it was her day job as a nanny to the wealthy, which allowed her to travel across the globe in search of photographic subjects, and curry such a philosophy.

Darger was a different story. He was a barely literate, mentally ill man who lived in a filthy apartment, worked as a janitor, mostly, and had a bizarre fantasy life that resulted in a terrible book called *In The Realms Of The Unreal*, the bulk of which is a work subtitled *The Story Of The Vivian Girls, In What Is Known As the Realms Of The Unreal, Of The Glandeco-Angelinian War Storm Caused By The Child Slave Rebellion*. I have read major parts of this, well.... I'll be generous and call it a *total mess*, when someone, 15 or more years ago, put portions of it online, only to have the vulturing *Estate of Darger* (a cabal of people that would have passed him by with scorn in real life) legally force its removal. I can affirm that it is a total *disasterpiece* on par with Ed Wood's film *Plan 9 From Outer Space*, and, in fact, much worse, as it lacks all humor that Wood's schlocky film possesses. Forget that Darger's atrocity has bad visual art and prose, for both of those aspects of the claimed 10+ million word illustrated work are not only terrible but wholly copied; but not in a transformative collage-like way. Darger literally traced cherubic-like little girls and other things from advertising works of the early 20th Century, and his lone change to make the work *transformative*, thus within the purview of Fair Use? Well, he added penises to the little girls because he likely never got close enough to and naked with a woman to know that they were not like men down below. Even worse is the prose which, when in his own *voice*, shows Darger as being barely above a child in intellect, while when copying whole texts of assorted prose from others within, shows no clarity, no understanding, and certainly no vision.

While Maier is a great artist, Darger is not even really an artist, in any true sense, although he has been held up as a political weapon by people to use to hammer the nation's arts institutes for insularity—a noble goal lost by doing so with a work of terrible art, if we grant it even that much. If Maier is indeed a great—and she is—then Darger is, at best, a demented (not *deranged*, as previously defined) curio whose work is better suited for studies in psychology and the brain, to determine how much non-socialization as a child played in Darger's mental ills—and not in any claims of supposed artistic greatness nor genius; outsider, weirdo, or not.

If you have read to this point, and seen Bruce's work, you can see that while Bruce shares obvious elements of his life with both Maier and Darger, he is clearly in the Maier camp in terms of excellence as an artist, and is as or more deserving than either of them in getting a major documentary made about him and his great art.

Like Darger, Bruce was mentally ill and could have easily fallen into the abysm of insanity, as Darger seems to have. Like Darger, Bruce did not take care of himself nor his domicile, and according to reports, did live in, if not filth, certainly less than a cleanly environment, despite both working as janitors for portions of their lives. Like Darger, Bruce thought of life in different ways, sometimes childishly, but he was able to transcend his differences in art, even moreso than in life. Like Darger, Bruce was similarly starved for love and recognition as an artist and person. But, like Maier, Bruce held down his own job, saved some money, owned a condo after securing a mortgage, socialized with a regular cast of acquaintances at the UPG, other arts groups, his church, his work, and online, and traveled to a handful of places about the world which, like Maier, made it into his poetic corpus—with some of them being art of the highest merit. This brings up the greatest and most essential tie that marks Bruce as more of modern poetry's Vivian Maier than Henry Darger, and that is the fact that he, like Maier, was great at his art form. And, to be honest, poetry is a far greater and harder form of art to be great in than still photography.

Another point that is cogent to my case for Bruce's status as a great poet is tied to his status as a weirdo poet/artist. As I have shown, despite Bruce's weirdness as a person and artist, and what that left in his poetry, 99% of his weird images, metaphors, lines, stanzas, and poems make sense—Negatively Capably—at end. Bruce is usually able to bring in the most far-out ideas and narratives from the ether and make them explicable to the percipient/reader.

This is not so with bad artists and poets, and not so with even merely solid to good artists and poets. The very fact that Bruce does this, and does it greatly at his best, and that this is a fundament of who he is as a person and poet, and what his work is as a body of literature, is the very essence of Negative Capability, the very product of his creative derangement, and a *sine qua non* of weirdo art and poetry!

But, neither Maier nor Darger were poets so was this a digression lost on the minds of readers? Not the best of you, but if some of you are untethered, let me toss back a lifeline and reel you back in. It is time to now look at some of the more noted weirdo poets in the English language canon, and compare them and their works to Bruce and his.

Emily Dickinson is likely the most famed weirdo poet in American history, and after initial underrating of her work, she is now one of the most overrated poets in world history, but she shares with Bruce a status, and that would be what I would call being an *anti-visionary*. When one speaks of visionary one usually means an artist or thinker whose works transform the way we think of the cosmos, and in a great and large way, as I mentioned earlier. But what of the person whose works are inwardly driven, and do not transform the cosmos, but draw the minds of others in like a black hole does to matter? This is the *anti-visionary*, and Dickinson fits the bill. Yet for all her quirky punctuation, the vast majority of her poems, even her great ones, suffer from an insularity, lack of depth, and that ill fated thing related to all of them sounding like the melody in *The Yellow Rose Of Texas*; things Bruce's greatest poems do not suffer from.

This untitled 8-line poem by Dickinson is one of her most famous, and it has all the flaws I mentioned:

> I'm Nobody! Who are you?
> Are you – Nobody – too?
> Then there's a pair of us!
> Don't tell! they'd advertise – you know!
>
> How dreary – to be – Somebody!
> How public – like a Frog –
> To tell one's name – the livelong June –
> To an admiring Bog!

Let us compare it to an untitled 5-line publishable ario—one that is not even titled *Untitled*—that deals with a similar crisis of selfness:

[Poem that may be a fragment of a longer poem – 2]

Surpassing its measure now
I see the pine bowing lowly
To the onward growth if humankind.
Finally I see the pine and me as one-
A combination of what is and what is to become.

Bruce's poem is clearly superior to Dickinson's. It's not as insular, it has more philosophic depth—note that the poem's last word is not the expected *come* but *become*—a far more active and transmogrifying word. Lastly it is well-alliterated and has sneaky internal rhymes that make it musical, but not overbearingly so, unlike Dickinson's far more predictable poem.

Let's see how these two weirdos philosophically deal with emotion in verse. First up is Dickinson, with another famed untitled poem on hope:

'Hope' is the thing with feathers –
That perches in the soul –
And sings the tune without the words –
And never stops – at all –

And sweetest – in the Gale – is heard –
And sore must be the storm –
That could abash the little Bird
That kept so many warm –

I've heard it in the chillest land –
And on the strangest Sea –
Yet – never – in Extremity,
It asked a crumb – of me.

Does this not have the flaws I previously ascribed to Dickinson's poems? Of course it does. Overlooked in the rush to restore Dickinson's poetry, with all its idiosyncrasies, is the fact that the majority of the punctuation restored is deleterious for the poem, both musically and emotionally, with its unneeded stops and starts. *Idiosyncrasy for idiosyncrasy's sake* does not magically make bad punctuation and music good, and this is Dickinson's major flaw as a poet, NOT that of her initial hack publishers nor restorers.

Here is Bruce's titleless publishable non-ario take on another emotion—remorse. And aside from both poems starting with the word of the emotions they will essay, Bruce's poem, a rare one with end-line rhymes, is again clearly superior to Dickinson's. His poem's music is not as thuddingly predictable, as he slips in an off rhyme in the poem's middle:

[Poem that may be a fragment of a longer poem – 1]

Remorse, heavy like a hard clod of earth,
Or a wingless airplane, or a snake's birth,
Is a vehicle I can raise muster
To overcome wanton, reckless lust.
I bow my head for a moment of peace
And sin trails off and I sense release.

Let's take on another paired set of poems from Dickinson and Bruce. Both deal with animals and being outside of oneself. Hers is another famed poem that fares a bit better than the others, as Dickinson's rhymes are not as predictable and dead on, nor is the poem's philosophy as trite and childish:

I heard a Fly buzz – when I died –
The Stillness in the Room
Was like the Stillness in the Air –
Between the Heaves of Storm –

The Eyes around – had wrung them dry –
And Breaths were gathering firm
For that last Onset – when the King
Be witnessed – in the Room –

I willed my Keepsakes – Signed away
What portion of me be
Assignable – and then it was
There interposed a Fly –

With Blue – uncertain – stumbling Buzz –
Between the light – and me –
And then the Windows failed – and then

I could not see to see –

Let's compare this with another publishable ario:

The Bull

Behind the gate, rider on my back
Tension high like a drum
I know what I'll do when I get over

To the other side of the fence.
I'll destroy him
Into little pieces

Run him around like a cyclone
Put him in a blender and spin it
Erupt this volcano

Walk him off a plank.

On first read this ario seems to not be as good as the other two prior ones we compared to Dickinson's poems, as it lacks the music seen before, but if we reread it we see that the poem is actually from the point of view of the bull! Yet, the bull seems somehow sentient in its knowledge of the human world and what it will do to rid itself of its rider—spin him in a blender? Walk him off a plank? While one could argue this pairing of poems favors Dickinson, Bruce does something that is very rare, if possibly nonexistent, in her poems, and that is to totally detach himself from himself. The 'I' in Bruce's poem is the bull, not Bruce, whereas the 'I' in Dickinson's poems is almost always her.

So, even when Bruce is not in top form and Dickinson is, Bruce can still offer more—at least in some parts and aspects—as a poet than she can. Partly this is a function of their lifetimes, art, and cultures being separated by over a century, but most of this is that Bruce, even in his ario form, was a far more diverse and greater poet than she was. I have already shown a diversity of subject matter, technical skill, and approaches that favor Bruce, and, as mentioned, excellence in quality, quantity, and diversity are the three hallmarks of greatness, and Bruce equals Dickinson in the first and easily surpasses her in the third. As for the second? Dickinson likely has more overall poems in her corpus, even if Bruce has a cache of poems yet to be discovered, but Bruce has far more poems of quality than Dickinson, as well as a great novel.

Let us now move on to a poet I have often favorably compared to Dickinson, and even claimed was her equal or superior, and that is Hazel Hall, an unfortunately obscure paraplegic poet who lived in the late 19th to early 20th Century and was a fan of Dickinson's verse. Her own poetry was not as oddly punctuated as Dickinson's, but its music was well superior. Like Bruce, Hall suffered from ills, although hers were more physical and less mental. Hall worked as a seamstress, even as she was confined to her family home. Here is a poem on her work that has a similar feel to Bruce's work poems:

Mending

Here are old things:
Fraying edges,
Ravelling threads;
And here are scraps of new goods,
Needles and thread,
An expectant thimble,
A pair of silver-toothed scissors.
Thimble on a finger,
New thread through an eye;
Needle, do not linger,
Hurry as you ply.
If you ever would be through
Hurry, scurry, fly!
Here are patches,
Felled edges,
Darned threads,
Strengthening old utility,
Pending the coming of the new.
Yes, I have been mending...
But also,
I have been enacting
A little travesty on life.

Note how Hall's poem (arguably her most well known and one of her best) focuses on the act of mending itself, and then ends with the poetic fillip at the end. Now compare that to Bruce's publishable non-ario:

Cleaning The Store

The cleaning vacuum sings along the carpet
And I am wheeling along
Almost doing nothing.

Each stroke
A spot of clean
And I move along

Until I'm done
And all of the dirt
Is trapped in my vacuum bag

And I've barely done a thing.

Bruce's poem, while shorter, has more repetition of words and ideas (doing/done) as well as better alliteration, even as each poem describes its speaker's acts. While both are fine poems I would argue that Bruce wrings more from less—a little more poesy technically and also in the description of the actions, plus Hall has to set up her ending by stepping back, exhaling, and then making her point, whereas Bruce's poem's point flows naturally from its form. There is no need to state directly, as if the rest of the poem has not worked. Also, what Hall states to end her poem is fairly hermetic—what is the travesty? That she has to work even while being handicapped? It's as if she is ashamed for mending, as if it is against the evolution of life, as she seems to state. It's a novel idea, but her ending structures it as if a grand revelation, not a natural consequence of the poem, and it simply does not live up to the buildup philosophically. Bruce's end posit, though is both a natural consequence of the poem's structure and philosophy to that point. Hall's poem is certainly an excellent one, but Bruce's is just a bit better, and more economical.

Here is another famed Hall poem:

Three Girls

Three school-girls pass this way each day:
Two of them go in the fluttery way
Of girls, with all that girlhood buys;
But one goes with a dream in her eyes,

Two of them have the eyes of girls
Whose hair is learning scorn of curls,
But the eyes of one are like wide doors
Opening out on misted shores.

And they will go as they go to-day
On to the end of life's short way;
Two will have what living buys,
And one will have the dream in her eyes.

Two will die as many must,
And fitly dust will welcome dust;
But dust has nothing to do with one –
She dies as soon as her dream is done.

This is an even better poem than the first of Hall's I used. It has a sing songy childish quality in its quatrains made of rhyming paired couplets, and this only increases the dread and horror, but it's a real existential horror about minorities, about difference, and about depth, and clearly Hall and Bruce would be the third girl, and this exceptional poem is framed by the narrator or speaker standing apart and aside (and above?) the young protagonists.

I will now present a publishable ario as counterpoint to Hall. While I think this poem just misses greatness when compared to Bruce's great arios, as I stated earlier this could very well be a great poem, and is the equal, at minimum, to Hall's poem, because I have used a harsher standard with Bruce's poems, as I have always done with my own poetry. With Hall and the others I have always been a bit more lax. Regardless, look how Bruce's ario achieves a similar end to Hall's poem without the child-like rhymes, and in less lines and words:

City People And Homes

The houses all look
So unique
Like individuals living there

As I imagine them
As the bus passes by.
The people with me on the bus,

Are city people.

They seem diverse – a dichotomy.
The two ways to see people

Means I must look through two eyes.

From Hall's poem's start she differentiates the one girl from the other two, and posits her as the superior—at least in some ways—maybe as the truly living party with free will and creativity. Bruce starts from the opposite end. His speaker notes the similarities of things and even states this is just his imagination. Bruce's poem then allows its enjambment to place the speaker in motion, looking at things as he passes. Hall's speaker is stationary as the girls pass. Hall's poem speaks of deeper things while grounded in the real. Bruce's poem is aware of the veneers—words like 'like,' 'imagine,' 'seem,' and then mentions young people. The young girls in Hall's poem are immediately noted at Hall's poem's start, whereas Bruce's people are differentiated as being of the city—as opposed to rural folks? Bruce then speaks of two ways to see people, yet both ways he notes are similar in that both are false—just 'seeming' and 'like.' Hall's poem's speaker speaks with no such awareness of falsities, and the poem's posit about differences, while well wrought, is expected because a) the rhyming quality presages that there is a lesson coming—it's like reading a fable and you know a lesson is in the offing, and b) because of the descriptions of the two girls and the outlier, you are not shocked by the poem's outcome. Now let's take a look at Bruce's poem's ending. Despite both ways of seeing the people within the bus and without, the speaker reaches a similar conclusion about them YET Bruce's poem turns inward, focusing on the speaker at the end, stating, 'The two ways to see people / Means I must look through two eyes.'

But, we all see through two eyes. Or is the difference between merely *seeing* and actively *looking* what is meant by this line? Or is it a comment on how the brain takes the parallax view of binocular vision and melds them into one, therefore the speaker is commenting on the need to sometimes not allow that to happen? While I could argue that Hall's poem is great, I can argue that Bruce's ario is even better, greater, and yet I don't list it with his so-called great arios. Why? Because they are even better than this poem, and while I am a believer in objectivity in life and art, Bruce's best poems are even better than the best of Hall and Dickinson because he is a greater poet, and has more great poetry than both of them combined. And so much so that the dividing line for Bruce's best poems is necessarily placed higher. Greatness has downsides like that—it expects more from the great artist than the lesser artist!

I have, in my own works, over the years, gotten many emails from people who rave over the greatness of poems that I do not consider such. This is where subjectivity comes in—not in denying all objectivity, but in stating that subjectivity is arguable in very qualitatively similar works, but objectivity reigns in most. The point is that I claim all is objective but so many, especially in the arts, claim that *all is subjective*, a ridiculous statement. Think of well noted bad films, like *Plan 9 From Outer Space* or *The Room*. Even average people can point out the obvious poor acting and other features. But, show them a technically well made bad film by Steven Spielberg and they cannot understand why mere bad writing, direction, nor acting can damn a good looking film. That is, they can accept objectivity when obvious, but not in the finer filigrees required to separate degrees of greatness or lesser quality. Hence, I state that Bruce's publishable ario is very likely a better poem than Hall's almost universally acclaimed great poem, but there is some room for argument.

What cannot be argued against is Bruce's greatness as a poet if his mere publishable work is equal to or greater than the great work of others, and clearly lesser than his own great poetry. Even his lesser quality poems are usually better than similar quality poems of others

I earlier mentioned William Carlos Williams, the master of laid-back free verse. Often lumped in with Imagist poets early on, Williams did expand beyond those confines. Let us look at one of Williams' most famous brief ario-like poems:

This Is Just To Say

I have eaten
the plums
that were in
the icebox

and which
you were probably

saving
for breakfast

Forgive me
they were delicious
so sweet
and so cold

Williams' poem is a *de facto* note left in the refrigerator to his wife
or someone else, and it is basically prose broken into 3 stanzas of 4
lines each. Enjambment is rather hell mell and the breaks do not add
to the poem. The only poetic *tack* used—other than no
punctuation—is that the poem's title is also its *de facto* first line.
Bruce's publishable ario does much more:

A Hint Of Happiness

This morning, on the way to work,
Amidst the tired
Travelers,

With openness,
Freely,
And very gaily,

A woman passenger
Told the busdriver
Some joke... some anecdote,

And my face warmed with a smile.

Here, the title is not part of the poem, but whose hint of happiness
is being referred to? The speaker's at seeing the poem's action? The
woman passenger? The busdriver? Also, note the good break at the
end of line 2, which drags us forward in the poem. Also note how
much more active Bruce's poem is. Williams' poem's action is all in
the past described in the note within the poem. Bruce's action is also
in the past, but it is in the past, on a bus, seen through the speaker's
eyes, of a woman doing something to another person. Bruce's poem,
in 2 less lines, is both more active and has more levels of depth. And
while joy ends both poems, Bruce's poem is the more interesting as,
even though the wording of the last line is not clever nor new, it

feels as genuine as Williams' poem does. And while Williams' poem is almost universally hailed as a great poem—one of the best short poems in English, Bruce's ario is easily its equal, and because it does much more, it is the superior poem, even though I don't classify it as one of Bruce's great arios. Again, like with Hall or Dickinson, I am taking what might be termed *second rate* Bruce poems and comparing them to poems acclaimed as great by most poetry critics, and Bruce, at minimum, holds his own, but, as I have shown, he can offer better and more complex and unique works than these *masters* of verse, these weirdo poets.

Now, let me turn to famed weirdo artist, painter, and poet e.e. cummings, whose most famed love poem, featured in Woody Allen's film *Hannah And Her Sisters*, is this untitled gem:

> somewhere i have never travelled,gladly beyond
> any experience,your eyes have their silence:
> in your most frail gesture are things which enclose me,
> or which i cannot touch because they are too near
>
> your slightest look easily will unclose me
> though i have closed myself as fingers,
> you open always petal by petal myself as Spring opens
> (touching skilfully,mysteriously)her first rose
>
> or if your wish be to close me, i and
> my life will shut very beautifully,suddenly,
> as when the heart of this flower imagines
> the snow carefully everywhere descending;
>
> nothing which we are to perceive in this world equals
> the power of your intense fragility:whose texture
> compels me with the color of its countries,
> rendering death and forever with each breathing
>
> (i do not know what it is about you that closes
> and opens;only something in me understands
> the voice of your eyes is deeper than all roses)
> nobody,not even the rain,has such small hands

Let me now offer up Bruce's great ario and love poem:

Creak

The thin line between your heart and mind
Is narrow like a choice
But written verse which swings.

Your mostly impregnable fortress repels most attempts
As if there were all the gold of the Pharoahs
At stake in your smile.

Won't you let me sing you a song?
I yearn to speak sweet everythings in your ear,
Take you for a trip into your dreams,

Allow me the creak of your heart.

Clearly cummings' poem is longer, mostly effusive, and bombards the reader with an overload of love images in a very Pablo Neruda (1904 – 1973) like way, and features many of cummings' stylistic choices—smooshed punctuations, no capitalization—and while this is also one of the great lyrics of the 20th Century, rife with great moments and imagery, it also has some trite images amongst the bounty: *eyes have their silence, open always petal by petal, her first rose, heart of this flower,* and *deeper than all roses.* None of these are fully inverted nor redeemed, but the fact that they are whelmed in three or more times the original and excellent images does moot their negative impact on the 20-line poem.

Now, let us examine what Bruce's great love poem does in half the lines. Bruce's poem does not offer a sensory overload, but delineates the emotional and intellectual aspects of love right away, then notes the narrowness of such, as emotion is always subject to the intellect. The claims that heart and mind differ is patently a false dichotomy, as without the mind emotions would not be as treasured enough to, oh, write poems about. Right? The speaker then further intellectualizes the love aspect by stating it is now part of the poem itself. Stanza 2 posits the beloved and wonders why he cannot get into her life. And the words 'impregnable fortress,' while familiar, is not a cliché, and certainly nothing as obviously trite as the 5 love poem clichés that cummings employs. Stanza 3 then has the speaker basically asking to be allowed to sing love to the beloved—or basically offer a love poem like cummings' and to then speak sweet *everythings*, not trite *nothings*, into the beloved's ear, and escort the beloved into dreams. This sets up the great end line, wherein the speaker, on the outside of love, simply pleads for a slight opening for love. Whereas cummings is loose, orgasmic, and not afraid to be schmaltzy, Bruce's poem has reservations, decorum, and no triteness. All banality has been intellectualized away so that the plea that ends the poem is loaded with emotional power, even as it is soft, and begs for a soft entry.

Now, cummings' love lyric is one of the great love poems of all times, but it is not a perfect poem—see my earlier delineation of perfect vs. great poems. That said, I am not going to claim that it is a lesser poem than Bruce's because they are so different. Bruce's poem is half as long, less orgasmic and musical, but it is also less trite, more unique (despite cummings' weird stylizations), and its ending is as great and memorable as cummings' poem through wholly different means.

Repeat after me: *Bruce Ario was a great poet!*

Let us now compare Bruce to Objectivist (and later Granny and weirdo) poet Lorine Niedecker (1903 – 1970), whose poems always remind me of the glass figurines in Tennessee Williams' play *The Glass Menagerie*. Here is one of her most well-known small poems, one with no title:

> There's a better shine
> on the pendulum
> than is on my hair
> and many times
>
> . . . .
>
> I've seen it there.

Let us compare that with a great ario—one which is a rare ario that, like Niedecker's poem, employs a whole poetic line made of punctuation:

> I'll Sign Off For Now
>
> Now much going on upstairs
> So I decided to pick up
> A new language.

A co-worker
Is Hearing impaired
Unable to communicate to me.

Taking the two conditions
Becoming aware
I decided to learn

_____!

Bruce's ario is nearly double the size of Niedecker's poem but Bruce's does so much more. First, its focus is outward not inward, and not rooted in vanity but the problems of another human being. Second, Niedecker's punctualized line is eliding what? A shine? And it is a line, not an ellipsis, as its placement is separated by a stanza break. Bruce's last line elides the sound of the world, as his elision stands for sign language, and cleverly harkens back to the title, and emphatically does so with an exclamation point! Niedecker's poem is, at best, a nice moment, whereas Bruce's poem is a great poem because it displaces the speaker and reader from a safe spot in a familiar medium, and does so without a second thought, as claimed in line 1. Bruce's poem also embodies real human care and not politically correct virtue signaling. Unlike Niedecker's poem—which is self-directed vanity.

Another well known Niedecker poem without a title:

Along the river
    wild sunflowers
over my head
    the dead
who gave me life
    give me this
our relative the air
    floods
our rich friend
    silt

This is a bit better than the last poem of hers, as it anthropomorphizes natural inanimate things, but, other than that it is almost imagistic in an H.D. (1886 – 1961) or William Carlos Williams way. Here is a publishable ario that evokes not only Niedecker but Williams:

Unbound

No seams or zippers
They've all been cast off
Like rain oil a windshield.

Pictures gone
Memories torn
Bare trees in the winter

Free to go
Shackles unclasped
Glass spilled

Dawn

It also reminds of Bruce's own lone great haiku:

Envious Feelings

Oriental Green
So I gave it some sunlight
To watch it grow out.

In both the ario and Niedecker poem nature overwhelms the mind of the speaker, but Bruce's overwhelm is total, as nothing of the speaker's self remains. Again, Bruce is a superior poet, even when his work is his less familiar and more stripped-down work.

Earlier I mentioned a weirdo poet and poem I would use in this essay, so here is the Weldon Kees poem I mentioned:

1926

The porchlight coming on again,
Early November, the dead leaves
Raked in piles, the wicker swing
Creaking. Across the lots
A phonograph is playing Ja-Da.

An orange moon. I see the lives
Of neighbors, mapped and marred
Like all the wars ahead, and R.
Insane, B. with his throat cut,
Fifteen years from now, in Omaha.

I did not know them then.
My airedale scratches at the door.
And I am back from seeing Milton Sills
And Doris Kenyon. Twelve years old.
The porchlight coming on again.

This is justly one of Kees' most famed and best poems. Kees was a poet known for his odd poems that had a very Edward Hopper-like feel to them, with characters that were somewhat misanthropic. But this one nails the genuine emotion of memory.

Let's look at this publishable ario:

Streetlight Night

The streetlight
Spots
The roadway.

I got my start
One night
Under a streetlight.

The brightness
Piercing
My inner darker mind.

I've never regretted streetlights at night.

Kees' poem overcomes its Norman Rockwell-like near clichés with the repetition of the porchlight as a warm glow into the past—almost like an episode of *The Twilight Zone*. Bruce's poem overcomes a near cliché in line 9 first by using the *-er* suffix twice to suggest something long buried (and perhaps as dark as Kees describes in his poem's second stanza?), then in line 10 with the odd declaration of never having regretted streetlights at night. As if anyone would? Or is the speaker using such a statement in a metaphorical sense, since stanza 2 harkens back to a past under streetlight where something in the speaker was begun? And the two poems do rely on the repetition of lights being stated.

Either way, Bruce's poem, in less lines and words, evokes as much as Kees' poem does, plus adding that great end line's odd claim as a different way to speak of and contextualize the past. At worst, the poems are equals. At best _____?

On to the next weirdo poet, and that is British poet Stevie Smith (1902 – 1971) and easily her most famous poem:

Not Waving But Drowning

Nobody heard him, the dead man,
But still he lay moaning:
I was much further out than you thought
And not waving but drowning.

Poor chap, he always loved larking
And now he's dead
It must have been too cold for him his heart gave way,
They said.

Oh, no no no, it was too cold always
(Still the dead one lay moaning)
I was much too far out all my life
And not waving but drowning.

This is a poem that relies on repetition, alliteration, and the displacement of a dead man's death by drowning to the speaker's metaphoric death in life. Now let's look at a remarkably similar take on such in a publishable ario by Bruce:

When It's Endless

Going under, drowning in an ocean
In the middle, no shore
Zapped, targeted, and isolated

A dive into yourself
With lead weights around your arms
Heavy, too heavy, very heavy

Nothing up only down, down
Fading lights out of reach
Graceless tired mire

Sinking, trying to swim, sinking.

Herein we also get drowning imagery, repetition, rhyme, and alliteration but whereas Smith's poem starts from without then pivots to within the speaker, Bruce's poem, which uses even more poetic techniques, is focused within, and to a literal drowning of the speaker. The difference is that Bruce's speaker's drowning is also likely metaphorical. It all depends on how one looks at the title and the period at poem's end. The period suggests finality—likely death, but the title can be read to imply this is a dream state that happens over and again and the period is just the finality of that *particular* dream moment, and it will happen once again. Of course, there may just be one literal drowning and the 'it' referred to in the title is death.

Either way, Bruce achieves a duplicity at his poem's end that is altogether different than the duplicity of metaphor Smith aims for. Yet again we see that a poem that is not even one of Bruce's best holds its own and then some against another poem almost universally hailed as great.

The next weirdo poet is Canadian bill bissett (1939 –), who has always been correctly viewed as a lesser e.e. cummings, right down to his lower-case nom de plume. bissett tries to go past cummings by including deliberate misspells of words in his verse and a total lack of punctuation, anticipating W.S. Merwin (1927 – 2019) and his non-intellectual punctuationless doggerel by over a decade.

Here is a fairly well-known sample of bissett's work, with a dedication, no less:

it usd 2 b
    4 konrad white n ken thomsod

yu cud get sum toilet papr
nd a newspapr both 4
a dollr fiftee

now yu cant   yu gotta
make a chois

Yes, a shitty poem literally on shit and its cost. But bissett is not even the weirdest poet Canada has produced. Here is an early *pome* by Wilfred Watson (1911 – 1998):

Pome Of Grief

Suddenly everybody burst into tears
As if the end of the world had come
And they were grieving
For all grieving done –
O bawl of wool –
And I did too,
For then all singing must be true

Note how the clichés used by Watson are just naked, and there is
not even an attempt to subvert them. Soon, however, Watson would
get even worse, devolving into what he called Number Grid Poetry,
such as this sample—the first stanza of a poem called *The Offshore
Canadians*:

my	1	father			
he	2	took			
			me	3	swimming
on	4	his			
			back	5	I
met	6	the			
			sea	7	at
		portsmouth		8	clinging
9	to				

Note how little effort and creativity it takes to do what bissett and
Watson do, but one need only again look above at Bruce's great ario,
I'll Sign Off For Now, and compare him to the 100% gimmick
poetry the two Canadians employ to see how Bruce towers over their
kiddy like verse and bad pseudorhymes. Let me then choose a
publishable ario on grief to compare to Watson's poem on the same
matter:

The Goodness Of Grief

Just as people need water and food
Nothing cleanses the soul like righteous grief
Not the despairing type but turnaround grief.

The kind that draws you to heaven
In awe of your vast limitations
And your penchant for balm

That heals fractured egos
And makes you whole
Ready for the fight

And sensitive to the mysteries behind masks.

Note how, after line 1's setup, we get the poem's longest line, with every next line shorter, as if the speaker is inhaling more quickly, before line 10's exhalation. We get the visual sense of the speaker tightening, drawing in on the pain from outside grief, and then acceptance and release. Is there any question that Bruce's poem is leagues above Watson's?

Not if you have been paying attention to this point.

Now, you might be thinking, ok, you have made and demonstrated claims for Bruce Ario's greatness as a poet, and you've even shown he is likely better than many famed weirdo poets, but how about non-weirdo poets, those poets closer to him in aspects other than weirdness?

Since I have claimed Bruce is THE Minneapolis poet, and, by extension, the best poet from Minnesota, why don't we take on Minnesota's most well known poet, the posthumously reviled and justly ridiculed Robert Bly (1926 – 2021); the man who helped spawn, and was the forefather of, the angry Trumper incel movement with his ridiculous 1990 Men's Rights Movement book, *Iron John*, a man who was the embodiment of whiny, wealthy, white men, and who spat on his youthful talent for fame and money, translating many bad foreign language poets into English, a man who was a fraud and knew he was fraud when confronted on it.

This poem is from this website: (https://tinyurl.com/3x8p8tsc):

The Cat In The Kitchen

Have you heard about the boy who walked by
The black water? I won't say much more.
Let's wait a few years. It wanted to be entered.
Sometimes a man walks by a pond, and a hand
Reaches out and pulls him in.

There was no
Intention, exactly. The pond was lonely, or needed
Calcium, bones would do. What happened then?

It was a little like the night wind, which is soft,
And moves slowly, sighing like an old woman
In her kitchen late at night, moving pans
About, lighting a fire, making some food for the cat.

The supposed thrust of this poem is to portray females as man-eaters—after all, water is the universal symbol for the female vs. the rock imagery of men. Hence, the cat of the poem is portrayed as some sort of she-devil that needs to be attended to by the man to fend off death. Is it a terrible poem? No, but it's certainly not good. There is no music to speak of, the imagery is trite, and there is no energy in the title nor last line. It just sort of sits there, a lumpenmenschen, not unlike what Bly was.

As I did with the weirdo poets, let's take a publishable non-ario to compare it to:

House Cat

The cat proudly struts
And I try
To get it under my spell.
But it has me
Under its.
Furball of an animal
It's a license to freedom.
For me
Who has this and that responsibility.
The cat knows
None.
It takes turn napping and eating
Watching life from open eyes.
Even when sleeping
It's not.
The cat has a heart.
I will search it out.
Maybe I will learn
How to be coy and oblivious at once.

Bruce's poem, while not great itself, is still well above Bly's poem. In Bruce's poem the cat's behaviors are not seen as a metaphor for trite female predation, but a thing to be admired by humans. Advantage, Bruce.

But, let us compare one of Bly's more lauded and famed poems to Bruce's work. This is from this website (https://tinyurl.com/jt8jxf8r):

Driving Toward The Lac Qui Parle River

I
I am driving; it is dusk; Minnesota.
The stubble field catches the last growth of sun.
The soybeans are breathing on all sides.
Old men are sitting before their houses on car seats
In the small towns. I am happy,
The moon rising above the turkey sheds.

II
The small world of the car
Plunges through the deep fields of the night,
On the road from Willmar to Milan.
This solitude covered with iron
Moves through the fields of night
Penetrated by the noise of crickets.

III
Nearly to Milan, suddenly a small bridge,
And water kneeling in the moonlight.
In small towns the houses are built right on the ground;
The lamplight falls on all fours on the grass.
When I reach the river, the full moon covers it.
A few people are talking, low, in a boat.

Is this a great poem? No. Is it bad? No, and it is better than the prior Bly poem even if the poem would be better by omitting the whole banal second part. So let us look at a poem that has a similar theme and end, even if it does not involve the speaker driving, as Bruce never drove after the accident which changed his life:

Out To The Store

I stepped out to the store
To get the vitamins
That the doctor wants me to take.

The glass danced in the windows of the shops,
Closed now at this later hour,
And cars flowed down the busy avenue.

On my way home from the store
I noticed the iciness of the sidewalk
And a small group of teenagers

Separating my business from theirs and the rest of the city.

Both speakers are out and going somewhere. Bly's speaker is
driving, Bruce's is going to a store. Bly's drives through metaphoric
clichés, Bruce's observes reality. Then to the similar endings: Bly's
speaker encounters his destination and some strangers talking too
low to be heard clearly, it seems. Bruce's speaker encounters some
teenagers who do as teens do, keep to themselves. But, compare the
actual last lines. Bly's is standard, rote, while Bruce's is an odd yet
interesting way to describe what his teenagers are doing. Again, in a
poem almost half the length, Bruce packs a wallop in his poem that
leaves a much more memorable moment and image.

Let's look at a lesser known, and even worse, Minneapolis poet
than Robert Bly: Michael Dennis Browne (1940 –), a former
professor at the University of Minnesota, and known about town, in
the 1990s, as the embodiment of the living dead white male poet and
a doggerelist. Browne specialized in ridiculously bad and cliché-
filled tripe that was never subverted nor redeemed the way Bruce
could do in his best poems worth publication. Browne literally had a
poem that started, 'The heart is a treasure box,' and it got worse after
that. Compare that laughable horror to a line like 'Allow me the
creak of your heart,' from Bruce's above great ario, *Creak*. Browne
often wrote poems of a page of more in length so I will just quote a
portion of a poem, *For The Young Men To Sing*, from his own
website (https://tinyurl.com/2s43e5cj):

It starts off like this:

we are all sons of fathers and mothers
we are all sons

singing

we are all rivers
the roar of waters

Yes, literally, in 5 lines and 21 words, Browne manages to tick off 5 clichés! And, again, this to open his poem!

After almost a page more of trite poetastry, the poem ends with this run of clichés, many of them highlighted in italics, showing Browne's utter cluelessness in regards to what triteness is and how it is the biggest bane of all art forms. He literally indulges in the worst of all possible ills:

> everything brimming in us
> everything dark in its barrel
>
> we are
>   *be*
> we are
>   *become*
> we are
>   *bless*
> we are
>   *dream*
>
> we are all sons
>
> *singing*

As I have done before, let me compare Browne's dreck with a publishable ario by Bruce, also about much the same subject matter:

In The Palm Of God's Hand

Through fields of grass and water
Over meadows, streams, and floods,
I have come.

Reading texts, singing hymns, and reciting prayers
Walking down lonely streets under the glow of a light
Rest in the palm.

I've searched, sought, swept clean
And still fought battles
Until I really heard

God's hand.

Now, by this point in the essay I should not have to point out why Bruce's poem is far superior to Browne's godawfully long poem, if not great. I mean, the very act of stating that one is singing in a poem, rather than actually singing in a poem, is bad enough, so I will just point out the wonderful synesthesia that end's Bruce's poem: *Until I really heard / God's hand.* Now look at Browne's end, again, and ask yourself how could an educated man, a professor with a six figure plus sinecure, actually write such terrible verse and think it is worth publishing? Then ask yourself how a mentally ill man with addictions and assorted other issues in his life could write so far superior a poem in a similar vein, and yet the dreck is what is published in the poets' lifetimes in university and high end poetry presses, while Bruce's achievement has to be published and bruited posthumously by me, another so-called *unpublished poet*, since Amazon publishing is not considered *real* publishing, regardless of the quality, a state that Bruce's art also inhabits.

I have railed for years about the cronyism and MFA Mafia in publishing and all arts, but can there be a starker example? Let me now give a side by side of a portion of Browne's dreck—an overly long poem called *Now We Belong*, and a similarly themed publishable ario by Bruce:

> Here are the rivers of many echoes,
>   Here are the leaves of every tree;
> Within us live the long horizons,
>   Winds that stir the sacred stones.
> Once we were strangers,
>   We were welcomed,
> Now we belong and believe in this land.

>   Keep faith, keep watch,
>   Take heart, take courage,
>   Guard mind, guard spirit.
>   Feed love, feed longing.

Then Summer

Take off that jacket, summer's here.
After a no-show on spring
I was awakened by summer.

Trees unholding their leaves
That must have appeared at night
Because weather was offish.

Sun shining just like I remembered it
Now thinking of new freedoms
Following from outdoor skies

That open my heart to warmth.

Both poems are about welcoming from the natural world, but Bruce's is not just a list poem of banalities, like Browne's. Bruce has interesting turns of phrase and images like 'Trees unholding their leaves,' and 'Because weather was offish.' Browne's poem is larded with 'long horizons' and 'once we were strangers,' among a handful more clichés. Yes, Bruce's endline, 'That open my heart to warmth,' is weak, and while that is important to note, the whole of Browne's poem, and that quoted, is ALL weakness!

I earlier mentioned how Bruce's car accident likely changed his mind so much that it made him a poet, and a great one. One wonders what sort of trauma could ever have made Browne think his poetic work—pure doggerel—had any worth to anyone or thing but his ego.

On to Lyle Daggett (1954 – 2018), both a weirdo and Minneapolis poet, and a loudly self-proclaimed communist, that of all those mentioned—weirdo or Minneapolitan, dead or alive, great or not—most resembled Bruce in many ways, even as he differed in many other ways. I met both of them at about the same time, and in the same local arts venues. They were almost perfect contemporaries. Bruce knew Daggett, and even attended Daggett's memorial; a thing Daggett would never have done had Bruce died first, as Daggett felt that religion was the enemy of the masses and often looked down upon Bruce for his Christianity.

Daggett always tried to make it seem as if *Lyle Daggett* was a name as well known as Robert Bly's. The truth is that Daggett's books were all published by vanity presses or presses owned by Daggett's friends and/or other communist-leaning types, such as Pemmican Press and Red Dragonfly Press, or presses that were Daggett's own creation—i.e., self published—like Shadow Press. Not that this is a bad thing, if the work merits it, as Bruce, Jess, and I publish via Amazon, a tool unavailable back at the turn of the century; but I will return to the literary aspect of Bruce vs. Daggett in a bit.

The things Bruce and Lyle shared were that they were poets, born a year apart, lived almost all their lives in Minneapolis, a few blocks apart, went to school locally, held longtime jobs, attended local poetry groups and readings, were slovenly, suffered from physical and mental ills that left them taking regimens of pills for their physical and mental ills every day, to ease their health issues, and they both died in their mid-60s.

But, other than that, Lyle and Bruce were the proverbial night and day in terms of personalities. Bruce was welcomed at all readings, whereas Lyle only ever went to a few select local readings, and never mixed with non-white poets. Bruce was well-liked—in fact, I can think of only one person who ever did not like Bruce—not Daggett, who merely tolerated Bruce, but a psychopath who did not like any of the UPGers, nor any of the local poets on the scene. Lyle was not well-liked, and as years went on he drew away from, or was shunned by, the local poetry scene, after numerous embarrassing incidents and confrontations with other poets and artists; the worst example being when he infamously got into an argument with a female writer who suffered from HIV, one night at a reading she hosted, after he went over the allotted time limit at the open mike and she asked him to let someone else onstage. Daggett raged and made a scene and, for the next year or so, he openly stalked and heckled this writer relentlessly at any reading she hosted. I recall one night, at the Coffee Gallery, where I had to intervene when Daggett would not allow this woman to speak and cruelly made remarks about her looks and so forth, and the cafe's owner asked Daggett to leave the premises. This was not the first nor last time Daggett took to heckling poets he did not like, as he made a regular practice of this at readings held in the Borders book shop in the Calhoun Square mall in Uptown Minneapolis, usually to those who disagreed with his politics. He tried that with me, once, but I easily embarrassed him in public and he never did that to me again. Others were not as lucky, nor quick witted with their tongue as I was, so Daggett continued his hecklings, usually the only one laughing at his own inane quips. This lasted until he was threatened with being banned from the store, after which he never returned to Borders. Daggett then largely withdrew from the poetry scene, at least until 2003, when Jess and I moved from the Twin Cities.

There were, as mentioned, the physical and mental ills both men endured, and the fact that both men were likely *incels* for the bulk of their lives, with Daggett being a virgin and Bruce only having experienced sex as a john in his 20s, at the height of his mental ills and addictions. As for their lack of sex and love, I have explained Bruce's reasons, even though he did date a handful of women for brief times over the three decades I knew him. Daggett's life problems were, in some ways, even worse than Bruce's. He was obese—about 5'8' tall and 350 or more pounds—and suffered from many ills caused by his morbid obesity, which was caused by his own addiction to junk food. Be it at work or at arts venues, I never did not see Daggett consuming massive amounts of junk food, likely a vain attempt to assuage his loneliness and bitterness. Whereas Bruce's slovenly nature, at the end of his life, which may have led to his life-ending accident, was a product of his mental ills alone, Daggett's filthy personal demeanor was a product of his mental ills plus his obesity, which made him very slow moving and fostered lesions and shingles like crusts on his body and extremities. I worked with Daggett for 5½ years in the AT&T collections department in downtown Minneapolis and he missed much time as a collections rep due to assorted problems he had with walking and heart issues. On top of that, as mentioned, Daggett's personal hygiene was deplorable. He always smelt badly, rarely bathed or cleaned his clothes, it seemed, and thus had dark stains all around the circumference of his belly and other private areas and was unkempt—never combed his balding and long, unruly hair. He wore eyeglasses with duct tape holding them together, and, except in winter, wore sandals that exposed his shingles-laden and unkempt feet and untrimmed toenails. Having an oily complexion, Daggett also suffered from facial acne and other such maladies. On top of his sickly appearance, and poor public behavior toward others, Daggett would be seen in public mauling his food, which became a sort of Minneapolis poetry scene in-joke, such as his need to tear apart junk food into smaller bits—be they muffins, bagels, or Oreo cookies—before eating them.

By contrast, after bottoming out, Bruce did try to rehabilitate his drug ravaged body, and became a long-distance runner, as well as taking martial arts classes. While neither man was a model of fitness, Bruce tried, and at about the same height as Daggett, he likely never weighed more than 200 pounds.

Daggett's unpleasant persona and mien had manifest repercussions to Daggett's degraded mental state, as much as Bruce's chemical addictions did to his. Whether at work or at public readings, Daggett was awash in tics—not *ticks*, but nervous bodily tics—involuntary reactions of his body to physical or emotional stress. Being around women (especially attractive ones, brought this to a head as his face would involuntarily contort and his eyes would blink beyond his control, and he would also stutter worse than he normally did. This would lead to a feedback loop where people would literally physically distance themselves from him, and often leave venues disgusted because he could not control his body's scent nor behaviors. This degree of odd public behavior was an area that Bruce did not suffer from. For all the woes Bruce went through in his life, once he got clean and sober, and on regular medication, such noxious public displays were in his past. This was not so with Daggett. In short, between his alienating appearance, his hostile actions toward other poets, and his tics and stuttering around women, Daggett made Bruce's problems, in some sense, seem minor.

Not that Bruce's issues really were minor, it is more that Bruce made a continuing effort to improve his life. Daggett did not. There was a certain arrogance that Daggett had, manifested in his disdain for Bruce's religion and his heckling of other poets, that Bruce never had. As mentioned, both men had to take many pills a day for mental and physical health issues. Bruce's were, as far as I know, mostly for mental ills, while Daggett took pills for his many mental *and* physical woes—those for high blood pressure, high cholesterol, diabetes, and a few other ills, as well as to contain his mental issues: anxieties, manic depression and some other ills. Other than costing both men lots of money for their medications, there were differences in both men's ills and actions regarding them. Bruce's mental ills after the car accident led him to a jail cell where he attempted to drink his own urine after an incident where he thought he was Jesus Christ and tried to get naked in the downtown Minneapolis skyway, among other colorfully odd episodes. But, other than a few passersby looking strangely at him, none of Bruce's mentally ill based actions hurt anyone but himself. The same is not so with Daggett.

There are two specific outflows of Daggett's mental woes that need mentioning as contrast to Bruce's, aside from his bad public behavior toward others. The first is that Daggett, because of his friendlessness, took up the tack of trying to be liked by others by claiming to be what was once known as being a *good man of the Left* in embracing, or at least mouthing, values that seemed to be in support or this or that rights drive by women, minorities, gays, etc., as a part of his claim that he was being a good communist. But, this claim at caring for others was another facade as, in fact, Daggett was not even a supporter of his own labor union, the Communications Workers of America (CWA) when, at the turn of the century, our local union was voting to go or not go on strike. Daggett opposed the strike, never attended a union meeting that I was at—and I was at most of them, and actively spoke against both the strike and union in the workplace, for inane reasons and those oft spouted by the company. This would be bad enough had he not been such an outspoken and self-professed communist and Marxist, but, even worse, was that Daggett was a loud and active apologist for, and denier of, the genocides in communist countries that left tens of millions dead, if not outright stating that he was a Stalinist or a Maoist; and he did not even really know what communism was. It was, for him, just a way to be a bit less of an outcast in late 20th Century America. Yet, when given the chance to actually stand against capitalism and corporatism, Daggett voted to NOT strike, and went against the very sorts of people his work always claimed to be in support of. This sort of hypocrisy was at the center of Daggett's soul, and a big difference from Bruce, who, for whatever his flaws, always tried to do what he could, even if he failed at a personal or professional level.

A few times over the years Daggett and I argued over his claimed communism and political positions and each time I had to reduce Daggett to a twitching, stuttering babble. Obviously these political views on unions and communism made Daggett a bit of an outcast and pariah in the arts scene, as well as within the collections office.

But that was not the worst example of what Daggett's mental ills produced in his antisocial behavior. Since the COVID-19 pandemic hit, awareness of the need for good personal hygiene, especially at the workplace, is higher than it was a couple of decades ago. Unfortunately, as I have stated, personal hygiene was never high on

Daggett's own personal list of priorities, and the incident I am going to relate is a perfect example of how mental ills can warp a person's mind to exact petty vengeances on individuals, and the world in general.

A few years after working together in the same AT&T collections office, Daggett joined the collections team I was on, and after a few months an incident happened, one day, that goes to the core of how some people with mental ills, like Daggett, react negatively to the world and others, like Bruce, react positively.

One afternoon, I had to go to the restroom. As I neared it I saw Daggett exiting the restroom and heading back to his cubicle. He did not see me as he was walking in the other direction. As I opened the restroom door handle I found that it and my hand were smeared in human feces. I recoiled, then went inside, washed my hands, and then washed the restroom door handle with wet paper towels. I washed my hands several times, urinated, then exited. When my team manager returned from lunch I went to talk to her of the feces incident, and told her this was a health risk, as we often had food days where people touched things each other brought in. I also mentioned Daggett's mental woes, which all people knew of, but not to the extent that I did. I worried that a public confrontation might send Daggett into some sort of suicidal spiral. The manager agreed, then asked me how she might best broach the subject. I had no real answers but warned her of the way he lashed out at poets he did not like, as she knew the two of us knew each other outside of work.

A couple weeks later my manager asked to speak to me, and then told me that she had raised the issue with upper management, and that Daggett had been spoken to. At the time I had thought that the incident was an accident, as Daggett's obesity resulted in dead, dried skin along the sides of his limbs, and that maybe he simply did not sense that he had left feces on his hands or arms. That's when the manager told me that it turned out that Daggett had been spoken to of similar incidents before, and that this had been a recurring problem. Still, nothing more came of it, save that the manager had to inform all the other collections reps of what happened on an individual basis. The end result was that no one would sit near Daggett, nor ever eat what he brought in on food days, and he was as clueless to this as he was in other areas, although he seemed to relish having his own junk food to eat on food days. Till the day he died,

Daggett had no clue that it was me whom he had literally shat on, as I never mentioned to him that it was me who had reported him. I had enough charity to worry over the psychological repercussions he might have had, but in the end it was all for naught, for here is the crux of the matter: when Daggett hit his lows, he kept on repeating his noxious behaviors, even if he compromised the feelings, health, or welfare of others. This is directly opposed to Bruce's behavior when he hit his lows: when Bruce landed in jail he resolved to change his life for the better, and did. Daggett did not. As for why Daggett did what he did regarding the feces I am reminded of a scene from the landmark television miniseries, *Roots*, wherein a slave named Kizzy encounters a white woman she grew up and played with. The white woman denies their past and a humiliated Kizzy spits in the cup of water she is ordered to fetch from the well. Daggett was a Kizzy, unable to lash out at the world physically, so his spreading of his feces, which he surely knew of, as it was a recurring thing, was his small way to get back at those in the world he felt had wronged him and owed him amends. Contrast that to Bruce, who had as much or more reasons to rail at the world, but chose a path of positivity. He never stalked, bullied, nor attacked others.

Of course, I mentioned that Daggett and Bruce were good comparisons in life and poetry, so, now that their lives have been compared, let us turn to their poetry. Things that Bruce and Daggett shared poetically was that they were both terrible critics of poetry, even their own, even as they both were capable of great poetry. I have discussed Bruce's canon, and I have read over 100 poems from Daggett's slim published output, as well as hearing that he read at readings, and I can say that Daggett had maybe 5 or 6 great poems (his best being a love ode called *It Droppeth As The Gentle Rain*), and maybe another 12 to 15 poems of good or better quality. Virtually all of the poems of quality he produced were Personalist poems. His political poems ranged from passable to outright doggerel, and like Bruce he could not distinguish the qualitative worth of the good nor bad poems from each other. Daggett always wrongly prized artistic intent over artistic accomplishment.

Unlike Bruce's short arios, and other poems, Daggett's poems were almost always longer than a page—often too long for their subject matter, and they would usually peter out as Daggett could not sustain the initial creative spark, and devolve into banalities and sloganeering as he would array lines meandering all over the page, with hit or miss placement, punctuation, and enjambment. Rhyme and alliteration were not valued in his free verse, and Daggett understood little of objectively breaking down a poem's mechanics, as he felt art was about political positions and feelings, not technique.

Daggett's lack of growth as a poet over the decades mirrored his lack of growth as a person (again an almost complete inverse of Bruce's growth as person and poet), and part of this was likely that most people (even me; see the above feces incident)—and our company—gave Daggett too many benefits of the doubt, rather than confronting him over his behaviors that were deleterious to others and himself, and forcing him to change. Hence, Daggett grew more and more isolated with time after every alienating incident of bad behavior. Contrast this to Bruce's active and engaged public life literally to his very last day of life, and the difference is clear. Similarly, Daggett's poetry, unlike Bruce's, grew staler, more repetitive, and worse with age—especially his political poetry.

Still, with all that being said, Daggett is the only real poet whom one might make an argument for as the true poet of Minneapolis, other than Bruce. I will thus compare the two of the poets' poems, but before I do, I need to allow Daggett's own words to damn his own artistic opinions.

This is my reply to Daggett's own inane claims on poetry, as documented (http://www.cosmoetica.com/B743-DES612.htm) on my website, Cosmoetica:

> Let us state here for the record that political correctness, understood properly, is a good thing.
>
> The expression 'politically correct' originally meant 'politically (and/or ethically/morally) the right thing to do.' It became a little confusing, sometimes, to talk about what was 'politically right' because it sounded a little bit like '*the* political right' (who are, of course, politically wrong). So people got into the habit of saying 'politically correct' instead, which sounded a little pompous sometimes but tended to be less confusing.

To write poetry with political content that is left-wing, working- class, populist, or of a similar nature, is the right thing to do.

The examples above make it clear that it is thoroughly possible to write poetry that has progressive political content and that is well-written. The fact is that left-wing political poetry, taken as a whole, is *better poetry* than poetry in which the poet has tried to leave politics out of it, or in which the poet has deliberately written from a right-wing perspective (I suppose a few examples of the latter do exist).

Daggett naturally leaves out all the social, political, and civil and human rights wrongs that PC has inflicted, then ends with the incredible claim that Left Wing poetry is, by virtue of its politics, better than Right Wing or apolitical poetry. Does he support this with even one aspect of the artistic, aesthetic, or craft-based understanding of the art form? Of course not. He simply declaims things:

Carl Sandburg wrote better poetry than Ezra Pound. Muriel Rukeyser wrote better poetry than T.S. Eliot.

Both cases are likely draws, and a ranking of the four poets would go: Sandburg, Pound, Eliot, Rukeyser- again, a draw.

Thomas McGrath wrote better poetry than Robert Lowell. Langston Hughes wrote better poetry than Wallace Stevens. Gwendolyn Brooks wrote better poetry than Marianne Moore.

In the first two cases, not even close. Lowell, a good man of the Left, by the way (just not Left enough for Daggett's ilk), was structurally and metaphorically better than McGrath, whose worst poems tended to ramble, whereas Lowell's retained their structure. Stevens was miles beyond Hughes. Hughes was a good versifier with a few real poems; Stevens was a master of music, idea, integration and juxtaposition. Brooks and Moore are close. The best of Brooks likely tops the best of Moore, but Brooks' last thirty years were devoted to writing horrid political poetry that lowers her overall oeuvre below that of Moore.

Mayakovsky wrote better poetry than Akhmatova or Mandelstam. Brecht wrote better poetry than Rilke. Otto René Castillo and Leonel Rugama wrote better poetry than Octavio Paz.

Although Akhmatova is overrated, Mandelstam is one of the few poets whose great poetry is translator-proof, while Mayakovsky's 'verse' is hilariously puerile, and he was a political hack. Brecht is not even a poet, he's a playwright- his verse is banal prose broken into lines, while Rilke is the only poet I've read with great poems in two languages (German and French), plus he has the most great poems of ant published poet I've ever read. I've not read Castillo, but Rugama is a typical Latino poetaster of the Left, while Paz is one of the two or three best poets to have ever written in Spanish.

> Etheridge Knight wrote better poetry than John Berryman. Sharon Doubiago and Joy Harjo and Dale Jacobson and Luis Rodríguez and Nellie Wong write better poetry than Jorie Graham or Marvin Bell or C. K. Williams or Billy Collins or Sharon Olds.

Berryman wrote one of the great long poems in American literature, and a number of other great poems, while Knight was a PC poetaster. Doubiago, who was a friend of Daggett's), and all the others are poetasters on par with the poetasters Daggett rips, so why even bother the comparison? Because Daggett has absolutely no aesthetic nor critical standard by which to base any of his claims.

> We don't need the ruling class (or its representatives in arts and letters) to tell us whether or not we're good poets. The record of our poetry, and the history from which it arises, speaks for itself. We reject 'literary' standards that preclude politics as acceptable or essential subject matter.

Again, Daggett is arguing against a straw man; claims no one has ever made; just his distorted ideas. The fact is that few people even care about poetry. Even Daggett, who writes it, and occasionally has thrown the dart that is a great poem, does not really care for poetry. By his own admission he sees it as only a means to an end, and a base one, at that: politics. Forget prostitution; is there any baser human activity than politics- the divvying up of power by the few over the many?

Now let us see Daggett's political poetry and compare it to Bruce's. This section from a Daggett poem called *Who Is This Man*:

> the president doesn't
> recognize his own hands. the
> ambassador from chase manhattan
> glances around nervously.

the fear they have created
has taken them over.

like a wind off the atlantic
it flows through the national
archives.
like dust it settles
on the shelves.

the president wakes up every
night, shivering, sweating.
he searches the air in
the room for movement,
for creatures with many legs.

This is a typical Daggett poem, in terms of form and political content. It lacks capitalization, it has a number of poorly enjambed lines, and the imagery and metaphor, especially at the end, is trite as can be. Is it as bad as Merwin's or Bly's verse? No, but it's not good.

Let us compare that to a slyly political publishable ario from Bruce:

Ghosts Behind The Wheel

It's 5:30, dark, and snowing and I'm walking along
But I can't see who's driving the metal shells
That drift down the road

Like husks of corn on a conveyor belt.
The corncobs will find their way home
And strip themselves of the outer layers

Until they appear as kernels
Like the truths they tell each other
Safe from the maddening snow

And a world knee-deep in lies.

Note how, literally, Bruce's very last line sums up and says more, and more effectively, than either Daggett's poem's selection or his whole poem! It has some excellent metaphors and images and the title gives nothing away regarding the powerful political comment on the zombie-like lives most people live.

Now, all of the Minneapolis poets I have compared Bruce to have been white males, you may say. Ok. Let me compare Bruce to a non-white PC Elitist Minneapolis poet who has long been affiliated with the terrible writing organization called *The Loft*. That is a Vietnamese slam poetaster named Thien-Bao Thuc-Phi (1975 –), who goes by the simpler nom de plume *Bao Phi*, but his work is, like Michael Dennis Browne's, uniformly bad and long, so I will just quote a piece of his bad long poem, *Therapist 4*, from his website (https://tinyurl.com/3u3f3dpa) and compare it to publishable arios by Bruce, one we've already seen before:

A river, wanting to go downhill
will carve new tributaries,
tear through homes,
flood the roots of trees.
The therapist tells you your mind
is swollen with doom
that carries you in its white rush,
torrents ripping through
rock and root.

Ice

Ice. The kind that makes you feel like a
   popsicle.
All over the streets. Manhandling the
   sidewalks.
Bitter. Cold.

The bus is way late
And I'm freezing
A hockey player out of the game.

I feel like a gerbil being tested in a lab
To see how much I can take
Or if I'll just solidify.

Reset. Somewhere a river flows and a
   bird sings.

So, in this ario-length segment of Bao Phi's poem we get the metaphor of nature to distill the speaker's mental ills, and that's all we get, as the section lacks music and engages in a few banalities. Bruce's ario, which we've tackled before, is not great, and its opening word is redundant, but note the metaphor of a gerbil that Bruce uses, and how he twists the animal testing motif into a uniquely Bruce-type moment, and then we get the flow of rivers which is not trite coming after such a unique 3rd stanza, rather than Bao Phi's immediate indulgence of such. And his stanza is set apart from the rest of the poem so it can be read as a *de facto* stand-alone poem. Nothing before presages it.

Later, Bao Phi's poem offers this stand-alone stanza:

At Minnehaha, a young Southeast Asian
  couple asked me
to take their picture.
Cambodian, or Lao, or Thai, or Viet.
He was heavily tattooed and looked like
  the dudes
who would have whooped my ass just
  for breathing,
back in the day.
She had dyed hair,
looked like the girls who dismissed me
as a pasty, boring little sellout back
  then.
They're the most gorgeous couple in the
  park.
If it sounds like I'm making
  assumptions about them and me,
I am,
and it's not okay
just because I'm Asian too.

Focusing On The Colors Of Summer

Blue river, bluer lakes, and bluest skies
Lush greens of leaves and the tall grass
Rainbows of flowers gardened in yards
  and parks

I might walk down a brown road in the
  country
Next to white fences
Sizing up red barns

In the city I walk down gray streets
Watching yellow, black, red, white,
  and brown
People circling
My summer of color.

Like many PC elitists, this horrible stanza lacks almost all technical skill, and relies on the slam poet's juking onstage and mimicking black rappers with hand movements—it's all in the performance, and not in the words. Then the damned stanza ends with the rebuke of self and foregrounding of the speaker's ethnicity. In both utterance and description, sentiment and lack of technique, the stanza—also *de facto* stand-alone poem—fails utterly.

Let's look at Bruce's take on race. He starts off noting the colors in natural things, then works his way up to the colors of human creations in a rural setting, then on to the city, where he lists colors, breaks a line, and reveals those colors to be those of humans, and they seem to be engaged in some sort of shamanistic motion about the speaker's world.

In a similar amount of words, Bruce simply allows the moment to be, knowing its power, while Bao Phi has to tell what his images and metaphors cannot convey in their triteness.

Now, the typical argument against my critique would be that I am not Vietnamese—or whatever social group is being lauded—so I cannot understand the basics of, say, bigotry or basic unfairness. That, of course, is ludicrous on the face of it, and makes imagination,

120

the central fire of all art, worthless, in both artist and percipient. And the poem is not subtle in waving its political bumper stickers, and bumper stickers are not subtle to begin with. Neither is Bao Phi, and this poem is a typical Bao Phi poem, just as Bruce's ario is typical of his canon.

Bruce is clearly well superior a poet to the Vietnamese doggerelist.

Maybe we should go even further afield from Bao Phi, to Amanda Gorman (1998 –), another PC Elitist poet who self identifies as a weirdo and had hearing and speech issues as a child; and who is a young black woman who was chosen to read a poem at President Biden's 2021 Inauguration, and who has been rewarded for reading her MFA doggerel at that event with publications of assorted poetry books and individual books with just a single poem in them, as well as a multi-million dollar deal from the Mattel toy company to produce a line of Amanda Gorman based Barbie dolls because.... well, apparently *Poetaster Barbie* is a thing, these days. Or is she *Hearing Impaired Barbie*? Or *Speech Disorder Barbie*? Maybe *Trifecta Barbie*? Regardless *Corporate Shill Barbie* may be the most accurate because that is what Gorman has become.

I will quote from two longer poems of hers printed in, of course, *The New Yorker*: (https://tinyurl.com/bdd2dby3).

Here is from the first one, with a terrible title, *Back To The Past*, and let's compare it to a publishable ario that deals with memory and suffering:

The closest we get to time travel Is our fears softening,	Took Up The Pen
	Sometime ago or was it last week… today?
Our hurts unclenching, As we become more akin	I decided to take up the pen Which means a lot of things
To kin, as we return To who we were	But not money, spotlights, or big houses More on the line of alleys, sunsets, and God, And a touch of bleary eyes
Before we actually were Anything or anyone—	
That is, when we were born unhating & unhindered, howling wetly	Broken spirits, uplifted hearts, chaotic minds
With everything we could yet become.	And words. Is it just words?

To travel back in time is to remember	Must be a combination of a lot
When all we knew of ourselves was love.	Don't forget the suffering part.

Gorman's poem snippet is larded with unredeemed clichés. This poem wallows in self-pity as the key to remembrance. Bruce's poem opens with a cloudy memory or not. It then delineates the material goods that Gorman embraces in her own life, and turns away from them to the realer things of quality, and only at the end, in one line does Bruce even mention suffering, and even then just as a reminder, whereas Gorman's poem ends in possibly the worst cliché she uses.

Is Bruce's a great poem? No, but it towers over Gorman's.

Another Gorman piece of dreck from a longer poem, *Ship's Manifest*, vs. the very same ario we just looked at:

This book is a message in a bottle.
This book is a letter.
This book does not let up.
This book is awake.
This book is a wake.
For what is a record but a reckoning?
The capsule captured?
A repository.
An ark articulated?
& the poet, the preserver
Of ghosts & gains,
Our demons & dreams,
Our haunts & hopes.
Here's to the preservation
Of a light so terrible.
	Took Up The Pen
	
	Sometime ago or was it last week…
	    today?
	I decided to take up the pen
	Which means a lot of things
	
	But not money, spotlights, or big
	    houses
	More on the line of alleys, sunsets, and
	    God,
	And a touch of bleary eyes
	
	Broken spirits, uplifted hearts, chaotic
	    minds
	And words. Is it just words?
	Must be a combination of a lot
	
	Don't forget the suffering part.

Gorman's poem is, as hard as it is to believe, even worse than the prior one. It's a simple listing of clichés as complaints. Bruce uses lists in his poem, but they play well off of each other, and, as with the first Gorman poem, her end here is terrible, an even worse cliché than before, whereas Bruce's ending is a turn from the negative toward recognition.

Gorman's work totally destroys the claims for Left Wing poetry that Daggett made, even more than Daggett's work. Even were one to compare Gorman's work to that of a black female poet, like Gwendolyn Brooks (1917 – 2000), it falls far short. Now, one may argue that Brooks lived a long and full life and Gorman is just starting out, at under a quarter century old, as of this writing, but whether compared to Brooks' juvenilia, her middle age poems in her poetic prime, or the later, worse 'jivey' street poems of her senescence, Gorman is behind her in all ways at all times, and shows not a hint of any real talent. Is Gorman the worst poet ever? No. The worst poet to read at an Inauguration? No. But her current published work should NOT be published. It is doggerel, pure and plainly.

But there are other reasons for her bad poetry to not be published and lauded, such as the promotion of bad art dumbs down culture, deadens minds, makes artists of real talent—especially the young—question why such palpably bad art is lauded, and if there is something wrong with *them* for clearly seeing the bad art for what it is. On a personal level, though, publishing her garbage hurts Gorman and other bad artists who do not deserve such promotion. How? It annihilates any incentive for her to improve. Likely, Gorman cannot improve, but let us say she could, and I am wrong, *why would she even try* to improve when she has learnt early on that she can get fame, plaudits, and millions of dollars just for spewing garbage? She has been taught what society values, so why change? In short, even were Gorman talented with words, this would stunt any growth. Lastly, it is manifestly unfair to actual great artists, poets like Bruce. Bruce worked 4 decades of hard manual labor. He contributed greatly to society with his art, and never got anything published by mainstream publishers, despite his greatness, nor would his bank account come close to what Gorman has already gotten for contributing nothing positive to society! And I know Bruce sent much of his work around to presses and literary agents only to get form rejection letters. In short, when great artists are not rewarded by society, and they are forced to spend large chunks of their lives doing uncreative and banal tasks to survive, society inevitably loses out on all the great works those artists could have made had they had more of their time devoted to said work, and not lost on work eager others, lacking any such talents, would be glad to do.

Is that right? No. And before one claims this is just bitterness, it is not. As I stated, the worst part of this is the dumbing down of culture, the alienating of the best of the best patrons and readers of the arts, not the fact that Bruce had to work jobs. But there is truth—that lauded commodity of the PC Elitist—in my nailing the very unfairness that this repository of great poetry by one of the Top 20 poets in the English language's history, namely Bruce Ario, could have been much longer and richer had Bruce been given the attention and reward that Gorman has gotten at the same age that Bruce had his terrible car accident. Imagine had Bruce not needed to work—might he have improved as a writer in other genres? Might he have 3 or 4 times the amount of great poetry he has? Might he have invented a 2nd or 3rd poetry form aside from the ario?

Gorman won't. I can guarantee she will not even come close to matching Bruce's output contained herein. Any and all motivation she may have had is gone, drowned in her millions. No, it's no loss to society since Gorman has no ability to do more, but for all the bad writers praised and rewarded—the Amanda Gormans and David Foster Wallaces and Maya Angelous and Robert Blys—there is a far more deserving writer that has been unfairly denied, and thus had their live and corpus of quality retarded.

Now, maybe you may wonder why I've stuck to weirdo and Minnesota and younger PC Elitist poets. Bruce was a 20th to 21st century white male, so how about comparing him to the same type from outside of Minnesota?

Ok, let us compare Bruce to the famed W.S. Merwin, a former U.S. Poet Laureate, and double Pulitzer Prize winner, who, like Robert Bly, had talent in his youth but then chucked it all away, spending the last 40+ years writing trite poems whose major *innovation* was....a lack of punctuation in his poems. Yes, *that's it!* It really sums up how utterly brainless most Academic poets have been in this down cycle of published poetic history. Merwin's verse became more and more simpleminded with every year and every book of doggerel he shat out. Bruce's work was deceptively simple, never simpleminded.

So, let us compare a part of a longer Merwin poem from this website (https://tinyurl.com/5srawpmn) with a publishable ario, and note that the writer of this article, a typical *New Yorker* poet named Dan Chiasson (1971 –), writes this of the Merwin poem quoted:

It took Merwin several volumes before arriving at a style barren and bleak enough to make his pronouncements on life's barrenness and bleakness feel persuasive. 'The Lice' (1967) was his breakthrough. It remains one of the indelible books about Vietnam: the images coming out of the war suggested, to Merwin, the utter defenselessness of a traditional culture against the fury of modernity. It seems to me that Merwin wanted these new poems to channel apocalyptic prophecy without suggesting that he was its source. Add punctuation to these lines from 'The Hydra,' and Merwin sounds like his Noah action figure. Strip it back out, and we have the distinct power of the poet at his finest'.

Oh, boy, we must be in for something quite good, right?

I was young and the dead were in other Ages
As the grass had its own language

Now I forget where the difference falls

One thing about the living sometimes a piece of us
Can stop dying for a moment
But you the dead

Once you go into those names you go on you never
Hesitate
You go on

Ok, so 5 or 6 clichés in 9 lines, and unlike in Bruce's poems, where he has clichés decontectualizing each other, these clichés are naked, and inert, and the poem also has bad enjambment. But, let us not forget that the poet Chiasson literally told us this was Merwin at his finest.... not employing punctuation in a raft of banalities.... *sigh*.
Now, Bruce's publishable ario:

Suppressing Mutiny

Light from a single focus enters the heart
Finding me like a needle
Possibilities of much but one path.

Every stray glance a blow
Bringing me to the brink

Of no return.

But I must return. Again and again.
Becoming comfortable with being uncomfortable
Leaning on resolve, a post

Looking not so much up or down – sideways

Bruce has a strong title and opening stanza, which mitigates the
weaker 2nd and 3rd stanzas. But stanza 3 ends well, and gives us a
great last line, one whose lack of punctuation at its end heightens the
poem, because looking sideways already implies a nonstandard take
on something that the lack of punctuation—namely a period—
underscores. In Merwin's poem the lack of a period follows a blatant
cliché. Bruce's poem is obviously the better one, even with some
flaws.

Let us now compare a full short poem of Merwin's
(https://tinyurl.com/y853kece) to another of Bruce's publishable
non-arios, and this time side by side:

Any Time

How long ago the day is
when at last I look at it
with the time it has taken
to be there still in it
now in the transparent light
with the flight in the voices
the beginning in the leaves
everything I remember
and before it before me
present at the speed of light
in the distance that I am
who keep reaching out to it
seeing all the time faster
where it has never stirred from
before there is anything
the darkness thinking the light

Snowfall Night

I take time to pause
From my hurried dream
To watch the snowflakes
Brushed from the window.
Snow is good.
Brings moisture in the Spring
It is cold but wet
Must be from heaven.
I watch the snowflakes
And indifferently they land
Spoken language
Knows not such beauty.

Merwin's poem is egregiously bad—at least a dozen clichés, and
unredeemed, in 16 lines. This is at Amanda Gorman or Michael
Dennis Browne or Bao Phi level....or worse! And the lack of
punctuation does nothing to enhance the poem's horror. Now look at

Bruce's 12-line effort. His title is specific, and for a reason- its speaker is not just farting out banalities but commenting on the setting of the title. Like Merwin, Bruce's poem lacks some punctuation, save at the end, but it's again not random. Look at both poem's last 3 lines. Merwin's is so bad it cannot be bettered with punctuation, and its lack does not improve the triteness. Let's look at Bruce's end: *And indifferently they land / Spoken language / Knows not such beauty.*

Let's compare two similar poems in theme and tone and quality— an arguably great English love sonnet, Sonnet 17 by Shakespeare, with a great love ario by Bruce, knowing that the ario is the closest thing to a free verse English sonnet there is, and keeping in mind that this ario is also a pre-UPG ario:

17

Who will believe my verse in time to come
If it were filled with your most high deserts?
Though yet, heaven knows, it is but as a tomb
Which hides your life and shows not half your parts.
If I could write the beauty of your eyes
And in fresh numbers number all your graces,
The age to come would say 'This poet lies;
Such heavenly touches ne'er touched earthly faces.'
So should my papers, yellowed with their age,
Be scorned, like old men of less truth than tongue,
And your true rights be termed a poet's rage
And stretchèd meter of an antique song.
  But were some child of yours alive that time,
  You should live twice—in it and in my rhyme.

Three Days In New York

The first end of it
Is the boardroom eyes
Perusing narrow sheets of typed paper.

Then time it takes us
Out to a comedy show
Riding in cabs fastly in the dark.

The touchdown, pinnacle, coup de grace
Is dinner with her in Greenwich Village.

We part with a kiss and a wave.

Three days past now but firm in memory.

Sonnet 17 is arguably a great poem, and I would claim it better than its more famous neighbor, Sonnet 18, which begins with the famed, *'Shall I compare thee to a summer's day?'* Note the naked clichés in Shakespeare's poem, in lines 5, 7, 12, and some less naked elsewhere, and how he mitigates, if not subverts, them and then ends up apostrophizing the beloved by stating he will be placing them in the sonnet.

First, the period at poem's ending makes us end definitively on that great endline and claim, which is both classical and clear, because while it might be trite in a love poem, despite its great phrasing, in this musing on nature it heightens the speaker's love of same. But the poem's end is not *de facto* the last two lines but the last three, as lines 10 and 11 can form two different sentences: 'And indifferently they land / Spoken' and 'And indifferently they land / Spoken language' and these two variants mean different things. And if we use the former version, then lines 11 and 12 can mean 'language / Knows not such beauty.' or 'Spoken language / Knows not such beauty.' These also have two different meanings and lend a duplicity and gravitas utterly not in Merwin's poem. Punctuation or not can make a difference. Merwin is clueless on this score.

Yet again, Bruce is a superior poet to Merwin, by a lot. And it's worth noting that almost all of Bruce's poems were out of his head. Many were bad, but the positives here just came to Bruce. That a poet claimed to be a master, like Merwin, and who supposedly worked hard on every word choice, who was lauded as much as a poet can be in this culture, can write such inane drivel, and a mentally ill man like Bruce can come up with an ending like he did, in a moment of clarity, shows not only how worthless Merwin and the MFA infrastructure in published writing is these days, but how great Bruce's mind was, even when not at its own best.

Is it not time for the bulk of poets and poetry lovers of quality to FLUSH all the shit of 75 years of published MFA workshop doggerel! You are one of those good poetry lovers, at minimum, if you have gotten this far and are reading these words: be angry and fuck the failed American publishing system! Criticize PC Elitist and

Dead White Male doggerel that suppresses real creativity in favor of bowdlerized banalities!

Now, you might think, well, I have not compared Bruce's poetry to old Dead White Male masters like.... oh, William Shakespeare.

So, let's do it.

Now look at Bruce's poem, and the first stanza declares a love now dead, but in stages, and sans banalities. In line 2 Bruce delineates 'boardroom eyes,' which clearly evoke the sexual 'bedroom eyes,' even as it comments on and critiques the very claim. Stanza 2 offers a second end, as if going through the motions, and the unusual choice of *fastly*, as if wanting to get it all over with. Stanza 3 then acts as a sort of false hope, a denial of what we have already been told of the love, and the last line—after the prior stanza's period and break enacts a small passage of time, places that past love, not in verse, but in memory. And line 10 makes great use of the duplicity created in the lack of punctuation it has. Yes, it ends in a period, but look at the word now, which if it only was referring to this very moment, would have commas before and after it. Lacking commas, it can be still read that way, but it can also, more ingeniously, be read as three days past *the now*, now as an ever-moving philosophic concept that separates the past and the future in the growing block universe of spacetime. This utterly displaces the percipient's sense of moment and makes the reality of the poem's present moment merely the future's memory. We are but the memories of things yet to be, and so forth.

Bruce's speaker is not overtly a poet, as is Shakespeare's, but Bruce is a better poet in this poem than Shakespeare is in his because he takes mostly non-love poem images and wrenches them for his own purposes, whereas Shakespeare rolls around in the genre, even as he transcends it with some great moments. Bruce's love poem, dealing with what comes after love, as well, is bold, lacking triteness, and less florid, yet just as powerful, especially at the end.

And these two poems bear out another reality; that art needs to advance and improve to stay capable of producing greatness. Bruce's poem has 4 centuries of philosophy, culture, and art on Shakespeare's sonnet, and it shows, as Bruce's poem engages in ideas and concepts not only unknown in Shakespeare's time, but unknowable, just my or Bruce's poems will necessarily have to seem limited compared to great poems written centuries hence, when interstellar travel, human evolution, and other wonders we can barely conceive of will be commonplace. If this does not happen, then society is stagnating. The very fact, therefore, that Bruce's love poem is superior to Shakespeare's is a **very** good thing, because it means 21st Century culture, warts and all, has advanced significantly beyond Shakespeare's time.

Let us turn to another famed Shakespeare love poem, Sonnet 109—also arguably near great yet not quite as good as Sonnet 17, and compare it to a great ario on love that I've already quoted before:

109

O, never say that I was false of heart,
Though absence seemed my flame to qualify;
As easy might I from myself depart
As from my soul, which in thy breast doth lie.
That is my home of love. If I have ranged,
Like him that travels I return again,
Just to the time, not with the time exchanged,
So that myself bring water for my stain.
Never believe, though in my nature reigned
All frailties that besiege all kinds of blood,
That it could so preposterously be stained
To leave for nothing all thy sum of good.
  For nothing this wide universe I call,
  Save thou, my rose; in it thou art my all.

Creak

The thin line between your heart and mind
Is narrow like a choice
But written verse which swings.

Your mostly impregnable fortress repels most attempts
As if there were all the gold of the Pharoahs
At stake in your smile.

Won't you let me sing you a song?
I yearn to speak sweet everythings in your ear,
Take you for a trip into your dreams,

Allow me the creak of your heart.

Sonnet 109 has some moments, but it is also clearly an inferior poem to Sonnet 17 with both its first and last lines being weak, and manifestly so. And there are more clichés within, as well. And like most Shakespeare love sonnets the apostrophes are a sort of cloak to hide the egoism of the sonnet's speaker.

This is not so in Bruce's love ario. The only verge into triteness is the first three words (thin lines, in general; *The Thin Blue Line*; *The Thin Red Line*, etc.), but line 2 utterly rehabilitates them with its unique phrasing and posit.

Now, some may say that the sonnets chosen are not Shakespeare's best, so I am biased and deliberately comparing lesser Shakespeare sonnets to great arios. I'd claim Shakespeare's two sonnets given are certainly among his best—and most critics would agree, and I would rank them in the near great category myself, as typical of Shakespeare's sonnets.

So, let me turn to the poet I consider the 17th Century's greatest English language poet, and certainly the best English language poet until Walt Whitman came along, and that is John Donne, an Anglican priest, whose verse is widely regarded as some of the best love poetry around. Take a look at his justly famed Holy Sonnet 14, and compare the energy in his poetry vs. Shakespeare's above:

> Batter my heart, three-person'd God, for you
> As yet but knock, breathe, shine, and seek to mend;
> That I may rise and stand, o'erthrow me, and bend
> Your force to break, blow, burn, and make me new.
> I, like an usurp'd town to another due,
> Labor to admit you, but oh, to no end;
> Reason, your viceroy in me, me should defend,
> But is captiv'd, and proves weak or untrue.
> Yet dearly I love you, and would be lov'd fain,
> But am betroth'd unto your enemy;
> Divorce me, untie or break that knot again,
> Take me to you, imprison me, for I,
> Except you enthrall me, never shall be free,
> Nor ever chaste, except you ravish me.

Certainly neither Shakespeare nor Bruce can match such overt passion, but Bruce is certainly closer to Donne than Shakespeare is with the uniqueness of his point of view, as well as phrasing in *Three*

Days In New York and *Creak*, than Shakespeare is with Sonnets 17 and 109. As I wrote earlier, I recall something said to me by a young Irish woman and poet, Laura Woods, who once told me that the reason John Donne is a better poet than Shakespeare is that every word Donne chooses seems absolutely organic and essential to his poem and line, whereas Shakespeare often just chose words to fill out a line or rhyme. And, if one thinks of it, that reason is the very reason that so many bad poets fall back on rhymes and other formal schema, because they cannot think of a word that sounds genuine for the moment—and that is the reality of art.

No one can claim that Donne willed Holy Sonnet 14 into being in just one mind's breath of a few minutes in length, but his speech reads *as if* it does. This is art, after all, and it is necessarily loaded with artifice. Art is not truth, all art is not truth, just as all art is not political, but it can be. Art tries to communicate things about reality that reality cannot do as well as art can. And art can be political, as long as the art is not subservient to the political. Then it is sloganeering. This ability to sound natural, in poesy and whether speaking of love or death or whatever, is a quality Shakespeare lacks, and the obvious clichés used in both of his sonnets, despite their otherwise excellence, is the very proof of Woods' claim of him and Donne. And Bruce's great love arios are certainly closer to Donne's sonnet, than Shakespeare's, in terms of triteness, or its lack.

Bruce Ario In The Poetry Canon

So where does Bruce Ario belong in both the English language poetry canon and the World poetry canon?

I have already delineated the issues with comparing translated poems with poems in their natal language, so let me take on the English language poetry canon first, and the best way to do so is to directly compare their relative quality, quantity, and diversity. I will stick with poets that are regularly bandied about in this canon, as I have disposed of many lesser poets in my poem-to-poem comparisons above.

The best method is to go chronologically. If we use Walt Whitman as the demarcation between Modern and Pre-Modern poets, who really stands out before Whitman as likely great poets, and how does Bruce compare to them?

Before Shakespeare there really is no one except for Geoffrey Chaucer (1340? – 1400), but *The Canterbury Tales*, while mostly written in verse, are known today more for their narratives than any exceptional poetic quality. The same can be said of *Beowulf*, making the Beowulf Poet less poet and more mythmaker.

63 or more great modern poems makes Bruce a greater poet than either.

What of the Bard, himself? Yes, technically one could argue his plays are poems, but most of his 37 plays are mediocre or bad, only a few are great, and only a dozen or two monologues could be taken out of context as stand-alone poems. His non-sonnet longer poems are quite bad and melodramatic. That leaves 8 to 12 great sonnets, maybe a few more, at best, and perhaps adding the 20 or so monologues as poems one gets to about half the number of great poems Bruce has. But, if not, Bruce is better, and by a wide margin. Split the difference and call it a draw, slightly leaning to Bruce.

I mentioned Donne as Shakespeare's superior, and the best pre-Whitman poet in English, as well as most daring, so logically that would seem to give Donne the edge; but, again, only if we give Donne props for sermons as poems, as we did Shakespeare for his plays, and hold Bruce to the more stringent 63 great poems, and not more that may be great. Like Shakespeare, I'll call it a draw, with perhaps a slight edge to Donne for his poems' holding up over centuries.

Who else? John Milton (1608 – 1674)? A few great small poems, and longer grossly overrated book-length poems. Bruce is better. William Wordsworth (1770 – 1850)? A dozen or so great sonnets, a few other longer poems, and lots and lots of lesser poems. No, Bruce is better. And one cannot compare the Trinity of Tragic Romantics with Bruce for they did not produce enough of quality for long enough. Hence, Bruce is better than Lord Byron (1788 – 1824), Percy Shelley (1792 – 1822), and John Keats (1795 – 1821). William Blake (1757 – 1827)? While he could be posited as a Whitman-like bottleneck, his verse is too hit and miss—some excellent childlike songs but too many overwrought and ill-thought-out vatic verses. One could argue that Bruce's arios are a sort of modern Blakean Songs, but they are better, and Bruce is better.

Walt Whitman? Ok, he has about as many as Bruce, likely, and much longer poems, which are harder to sustain greatness in, so, pre-Whitman I can only really give Donne the edge. Whitman makes 2, so, against published major male poets (discounting myself, Jessica, and Don Moss—his 'unpublished' great contemporaries), that makes Bruce no worse than 3rd in the English language.

I have shown Bruce's superiority to Dickinson and Hazel Hall, so what of other female poets in the canon? A grossly overlooked poet is Elizabeth Barrett Browning (1806 – 1861)—much better than her husband, and whose sonnets are superior to Shakespeare's in quality and number, and who has an actually great novel in verse, *Aurora Leigh*. That's enough to put her in the Bruce, Donne, Shakespeare range, and arguably slightly better than Bruce, so let's say Bruce is 3rd or 4th now. Edna St. Vincent Millay (1892 – 1950) has even more great sonnets (3 or more dozen?) than Browning, lacks the novel in verse, but has a number of great longer poems, so let us put her in that cluster and say Bruce is between #3 and #5, at worst. Sylvia Plath has about half the great poems Bruce does, but they are longer and more daring, and Australia's Judith Wright (1915 – 2000) is in a similar place as Plath, so, at worst, Bruce is #7. At worst, he's #10 if we grant the obvious—that Wallace Stevens bests him with dozens of longer, daring philosophical poems; Hart Crane bests him with 20 or more longer great poems and the greatest book-length poem in the English language, *The Bridge*; and Robinson Jeffers bests Bruce with long vatic poems that look Whitmanian, if more daring, and with a number of great long-book length poems.

Carl Sandburg also wrote a few great long poetic pieces, a very good book-length poem, as well as quite a few shorter Bruce-like poems—in terms of style and philosophy—and he might be the closest antecedent to Bruce's poetic work; so he's arguably equal or better than Bruce. Robert Frost is in that muddle with Donne and Bruce and Plath and company. At worst, Bruce is thus #12. What of that trinity of early Modernists? T.S. Eliot, Ezra Pound (1885 – 1972), and W.B. Yeats (1865 – 1939) simply don't have enough great poems to compare to Bruce—especially Pound and Eliot.

Who else? How about 20th Century name poets like Robert Lowell (1917 – 1977), John Berryman (1914 – 1972), Charles Olson (1910 – 1970), Kenneth Rexroth (1905 – 1982), Kenneth Patchen (1911 – 1972), and Allen Ginsberg (1926 – 1997)? No, not a one has more than 12 to 15 great poems, although one might make arguments for Berryman's and Olson's book-length poems, but their best stuff in those books is also mired in much lesser stuff, as well. In the U.K. there simply is no other poet that even reaches the statures of the poets just mentioned. The same can be said for any other Canadian, Australian, New Zealander, nor any other English-speaking poets.

That leaves Americans, and there are no great minority American poets save for a few black poets, but none of them have the numbers of great poems to displace Bruce from such a list. That includes Robert Hayden, Gwendolyn Brooks, James Emanuel, Countee Cullen, and Langston Hughes (1901 – 1967).

By my reckon, that means in his native language, Bruce is no worse than the 12th best poet, and arguably as high as #6, with only Donne, Whitman, Stevens, Jeffers, and Crane as clearly better. In the mix with Bruce are E.B. Browning, Millay, Plath, Wright, Sandburg, and Frost. If one wants to add Shakespeare that means between 6th and 13th on such a list. Add in Jessica, with a similar number of great poems, more diversity, and likely more years to add to her number; add in Don Moss with 15 or so great smaller poems and his book-length *Dominions*; and me, and 7th to 16th is the range Bruce Ario resides in as a published English language poet.

Not bad for a man who suffered from assorted mental ills and addictions for decades!

As for other languages, one might claim Boris Pasternak, Osip Mandelstam (1891 – 1938), and Marina Tsvetaeva (1892 – 1941) in Russian, Rilke and maybe J.W von Goethe (1749 – 1832) in German, Charles Baudelaire (1821 – 1867) in French, Petrarch (1304 – 1374) and Dante (1265 – 1321) in Italian—Giovanni Boccaccio (1313 – 1375) does not make it for he is Italy's answer to Chaucer—more famed for the narratives than poesy in his verse—and maybe a handful of Spanish language poets like Pablo Neruda, Octavio Paz (1914 – 1998), Vicente Huidobro (1893 – 1948), maybe Nazim Hikmet (1902 – 1963) in Turkish, and maybe another handful I've never read, or overlooked. So worldwide, let's say half of those 17, at best, are better than Bruce, so that's 8 or 9, which means Bruce ranks between 15th and 22nd if included with major published poets, and 16th to 25th if I, Jess, and Don Moss are included.

Again, this is all from a man who was once a homeless raving maniac you'd pass by in any typical big American city.

Conclusion

I stated that I was here to introduce Bruce Ario to the average poetry reader and to the pantheon of great poets. I have done so and have shown the overall quality of Bruce Ario's poetic corpus on its own, via the tools of the trade, and Bruce's greatness as a poet should be blatantly obvious to anyone remotely familiar with the art form. I don't say he is a great poet because he was my friend and I want to booster him, just as I do not laud Don Moss's *Dominions* as the greatest book-length poem in English this side of *The Bridge* because he is my friend, nor laud Jessica's poetry because she is my wife. As with Bruce, any perusal of Don's and Jess's work makes their greatness plain. It should not have to be pointed out to the frauds who run MFA writing mills nor the publishing industry, but I have done it. I have shown how even many of Bruce's second tier works are the equal or superior of many works bruited as great by critics over the centuries. Of course, as with all poets, I am displaying Bruce at his best. In the bulk of Bruce's poetic corpus I have included perhaps as little as 40 or 50% of his actually produced and/or currently known work—most of it of unpublishable quality. I may discover later works that he published online in his self-published Amazon books, or maybe poems he had on old computer drives, and, as mentioned, there is a chance that some poems (*who knows how many?*) were inadvertently lost due to years of Bruce's own neglect in protecting his work and/or parts of his corpus being tossed in the trash after his death, when people were hired to clean out his living space, again due to his own neglect.

But, as I type these words, just a few months after Bruce's death, his 46 great arios, his 54 great poems overall, out of 378 so far canonical poems, in this volume, no matter how seemingly slight compared to long or book length poems, is an achievement that, as I demonstrated above, ranks Bruce Ario in the Top 20 or 25 of English language poets of all time, minimum. The sheer volume of his verse cannot be denied, nor can his greatness.

Bruce was a true working-class poet and artist, unfettered by PC and MFA constraints, and this and his greatness is why I have been so forceful in my arguments pro-Bruce's poems. I do art as contact sport when it is needed, and wipe the floor with phonies like Robert

Bly, Donald Hall (1928 – 2018), and Amiri Baraka (1934 – 2014). Bruce was never one to prostitute his mental ills and pains to score sympathy for his poems. He just did them, and read them. He was not like Robert Bly, someone to squander his talent and advocate for the ridiculous and misogynistic Men's Rights Movement. Bruce was not selfish nor a bigot. He was not like Donald Hall, who cynically, after the death of his poetaster wife, Jane Kenyon (1947 – 1995), wrote a bad book of poems about her, then cried on cue to sell copies of the book at readings. Bruce was not so cynical and pelf-driven. He was not like Amiri Baraka, who used his fame to score with white co-eds. Bruce was not a hypocrite. Bruce was a better person and poet, and wrote more great poems than all 3 of them combined.

But know this—writing and language, and literature, the art form of the two tasks mentioned, is by far the single hardest task any human being can do. It is the highest generic art and poetry is the highest specific form of that art because, lacking telepathy, written squiggles on a medium is the closest we can get to telepathic art. And unlike other art forms, literature and poetry invite percipient participation and co-creation. Your Captain Ahab or Anne Shirley will surely look different than anyone else's, no matter how closely described. The motivations of Sancho Panza or Biff Loman will vary due to your or her interpretation.

Why is this?

It is because art forms based on aural or visual means have it easy. It is much easier to move someone with a weeping violin or a good beat because ears and hearing have been around for 600 or more million years. We are literally all evolutionarily and genetically hardwired to have tremendous reactions to sound because it could be coming from a predator wanting to kill and eat us. The same is true for paintings, sculpture, photography and cinema, because, like ears, we have had eyes for nigh a billion years, and we are alive because all of our ancestors, back to the literal first one with eyes, used those eyes just well enough to produce offspring who used their eyes well enough to produce offspring, and so we are beneficiaries of such visual abilities and respond to it instinctually. Even performing arts depend on the human brain's evolved mammalian need for play to keep it fresh.

In truth, the only current art form we have that is wholly cut off from the sensory world, and comes about generated from within, is that of language, which is perhaps 200,000 years old, and written language, which maybe goes back 6 to 10 thousand years, depending on how you reckon such. Either way, literature is an artistic infant, and an almost entirely mindly art form, and yet it does so much—it moves us like no other art form. Damn Virtual Reality, literature is the ultimate Virtual Reality maker, and you are far more in control of it than that claimed by computer algorithms. Literature does the most with the least of any human art form, and any human endeavor. We recall baby rhymes, characters in children's books, adventures, heroes, villains, strong women, clever men, that boy who once read a bad love poem he wrote to ask you out, that snippet of a Holy Book that made you think, and so on.

10 thousand years versus 600 million to a billion years. Yes, literature is an art form like no other—one gets the most from the least, in a sensual and stimulative sense, and its great practitioners are so often dismissed by the masses. A friend of mine once said, 'Everyone thinks they can write because all you need is a paper and pencil.' It's true. No one thinks they can be Vermeer nor Kubrick because they used to take Polaroids. No one thinks they are Bach nor Led Zeppelin just because they can whistle a tune. But most people have no such qualms nor reservations about writing. It's how the Wilfred Watsons, Michael Dennis Brownes, and Amanda Gormans come about.

So what of the truly great?—not only those ensconced in the canon alongside those without merit, but the truly great, like Bruce? Why are the great made to be outsiders? Why does this damnable *deliterate*—i.e., the active choice to not read great works of literature—culture not have the people nor infrastructure to allow its greatest art form to flourish by putting forth the greatest poets to be read and admired, not frauds like Watson, not careerist hacks like Browne, not lazy, lousy, but lauded tokens like Gorman?

There is a need to change this culture that does not reward great artists in a society that scorns and damns and belittles artists who even dare to be great much less are, like Bruce, Jess, me, Don Moss, and even James Emanuel, who was published by the system and now is mostly forgotten in his native country of America.

This book is another weapon in that battle. Bruce Ario was a great poet, and that he was, and attained such a level in the pantheon of American poetry, is testament to his hard work, to overcome his mental illnesses, and his success, even though he had much less than many far more naturally gifted people with higher initial ceilings. He may be an outsider to the MFA Mafia, the idiots in charge of publishing houses, but he is a poet who stands above many of the poets I name within.

Please, help change the artistic world in the smallest way possible. Buy this book and understand why Bruce was a great poet, tell others, encourage the sale of the book—not only for art's sake, which is a good enough reason, but because whatever meager proceeds are made by this book's publication will go not to me nor the Estate of Bruce Ario, but to two of Bruce's favorite causes, his church and his workplace.

In closing, let me state that this is not the final word on Bruce Ario, the poet. I do plan on scouring Bruce's computer and self-published Amazon books, and if I find enough work of quality I shall include said poems in the aforementioned later edition of this work, a *Final Poems*. Someone else can do Bruce's *Collected* or *Complete Poems* down the line.

As for Bruce's journalism, work articles, plays, novels aside from a restored and unbowdlerized version of *Cityboy*, those too may have to wait for another set of dispassionate eyes, as will any biographies of Bruce's life, parts of which will be found in online interviews with and about the man at the Cosmoetica and Automachination YouTube channels. Jessica suggests that the best title for any biography on Bruce would be wise to reuse the title of one of his greatest arios, *Just As It Was*:

> The moon isn't quite the way it was
> Last month it was over there
> And it seemed lighter in the sky.
>
> But I'm on the same bus bench
> As I have been for some time now
> Whether tonight or the last 30 years.
>
> Change seems so difficult
> Genuine change
> Anybody can change clothes
>
> But few can move the moon from there to there.

Yeah, that's great! To paraphrase early American baseball star Babe Ruth, after he hit 60 home runs in one season, apropos of a mentally ill man's ability to produce at least 63 great poems in his lifetime: '63, let some bastard top that!'

Dan Schneider, www.Cosmoetica.com
Autumn, 2022

*****

Please contact me, Dan Schneider, Bruce Ario's literary executor, at any of my online venues, for any permissions for projects on poems, books, videos, and films on the life of Bruce Ario; or if you want to send, or know of where to find any more of Bruce's lost poems, like *What Shadow?*, online or off.

Selected Poems

PUBLISHER'S NOTE

Bruce Ario often had typographical quirks in his poetry, including the inconsistent use of hyphens and dashes, quotation marks, spacing, and more. There are often varying forms of each, reflecting his use of different typewriters and word processing applications over the years. Except in the case of obvious typos and unreadability, these quirks have been preserved to reflect his idiosyncrasies. Many poems likewise have multiple noncanonical versions.

Great Non-Arios – 8 poems

In Brief

The brevity of life
Ticks in my watch
Slapped on my left wrist
And I pick up the pace
Then slow down
To see the Phillips screws on the machines.
Somewhere a cat meows
Longing for attention.
I stand unadorned
Ashamed and half broken-hearted.
Before I die I must go back,
Back to a spot which may have never been.
Clearly it is a time of warning
For me who dreamed endlessly.
The rosebushes are covered;
It's winter out there.
Someone's telling me,
'Live for today.'
I must collect, always collect
Myself who spins like everyone else.

The Lovely Tree Branches

Frail tree limbs a delicate adventure
To watch closely into the night
When the city is so still
And all that is around me slumbers.
I can't forsake the mission
In my heart which breathes air
Against hustle bustle sleepers
Who are juxtaposed in a dream
Near the limbs not quite on them
No the limbs are almost bare of anything human
Except for the open eyed woman.
I saw her just yesterday in her shawl
Moving ever so close to the lovely tree branches.

Grandma

> I talked to you last Friday night
> And then you were gone.
>
> The snow looks so white;
> It's chilly outside.
>
> No more phone calls...

No more

admonitions, stories, or worries... secrets.
> All of my thoughts trail off
> From a loving memory.
> You were there when I needed you
> You are where you need to be now.
> It isn't goodbye
> Because death turns to a new relationship...
> You are 98 years old and growing

upward.

touch

light

your

trace

I

Your gentle ways pass on…

Ring

The young man saunters into the craftsman's shop
Lured by a sign advertising jewelry.
He buys a ring with no knowledge why.
Maybe it catches some fancy or will have purpose.
His parents are casting a similar ring
Which fits around his finger invisibly.
He has hunted it down by the river,
In a crowd downtown, and on girls' hands.
The hardness of the shop's ring
Holds the young man's curious look.
It's a whim passing through his mind like weather
While his parents' ring is like a carrot before him.
The shop ring reminds him
Of a woman he's known or someone he hasn't met.
He walks home to show it to his parents
Who joyfully see it and see their ring across his forehead.

Envious Feelings

Oriental Green
So I gave it some sunlight
To watch it grow out.

Running Away With Clothes

I've always liked the luster of clothes
Hiding our nakedness
And so much more.

Or do they enhance
Our walk from the Garden of Eden
Spread out in trousers or skirts?

Adam and Eve wore figs
And I - a pair of jeans
Which shows me something

About my nature
And men's and women's
And confusion over the two

Like me experimenting
And stopping just short
Of cowboy boots

With styles so diverse
Yet hiding me
Like a cloak in the closet

Even though since my youth
It was the most natural
Way to go:

To attire myself.
I won't spend a lot of money
Or time...

Clothes... Where did they come from?

Urban Walkways

Sidewalks may catch my stride
In a jog or just a stroll
Any day of the week
As the time bides.

Weather permitting or not
I take my cause to their paths
Perhaps with no permission
Other than the life I've got.

Point A to point B -
That's sidewalk 1 to sidewalk 2
Perpendiculars
Then across on 3.

Asphalt, cement, new and old
Our sidewalks come in differing shape,
Form. Narrow notebooks of our feet,
Or strands or veins of the fold.

Signature

My signature came to me
When I came into this life
At the hospital
Without much else mine.

In third grade, Mrs Johnson
Taught me how to write my signature
in nice fashion
With my own fountain pen.

By high school, I was experimenting with my signature
Determined to find the right way to do it.

In college, my signature flew off the paper
And into my mind where it stayed.

Now as an adult I have my signature close to my heart
And it does special things for me.
It portrays.
It relays.
And it delays.
My signature portrays all that
Business, stature, and word of honor require.
My signature relays all that I was -
That is lodged firmly in my mind.
Finally, my signature delays
What could otherwise be slow death
From an unsigned life.

Publishable Non-Arios – 59 poems

Moments

Cat

Creation's jewel of joy
Given to me in this feline playmate
Who prances through doors
And struts down highways
Like it is possible she's in charge
And not me, who spends much money on her food and
housing.

House Cat

The cat proudly struts
And I try
To get it under my spell.
But it has me
Under its.
Furball of an animal
It's a license to freedom.
For me
Who has this and that responsibility.
The cat knows
None.
It takes turn napping and eating
Watching life from open eyes.
Even when sleeping
It's not.
The cat has a heart.
I will search it out.
Maybe I will learn
How to be coy and oblivious at once.

Untitled (1)

The plant is in the corner
Set there sometime in the past
By one who is a Spring mourner
To stay with us this Winter and last.
It has its place today and tomorrow
It's in a series of nature's gifts
That I look to and borrow
To give my spirit needed lifts.
Green leaves stand up sprightly
My attention's to the demeanor
Of the plant in the light
Content to live out this season leaner
Than other plants in Spring so full.
Though Winter howls like a wolf
My eyes light on it, the walls mull
The plant stands straight and aloof.

Trickle Of Ice In July

There still is a trickle of ice in my bones
Even though it's way past winter and into July.
It just hasn't stopped raining for so long
That I haven't gotten a chance to warm up and enjoy
summer.
Winter left a trickle of ice in my life
Causing me to shiver and my soul to quake.
I'm not uneasy or panicky-
Just a little cold because of winter and all.

Fall Day

All the leaves are gone.
I brace myself for what's to come.
It was a short sweet Fall;
My hair is short and disheveled.
And my head is cold.
We lumber on! Fall and I.
The sunsets press on the afternoons.
My jog is almost nice.
Leaves are gone;
The trees blend with the wind.
I will entertain thoughts of Winter.
The leaves from the trees are gone.

Night Plays On

The night plays gentle music
With crickets singing in rhythm.
Inside the house I bear my life
Like a candle in the dark.
The blackness of the morning
Looks to me like death
When I might lie down forever
To a different sensation.
The open windows let night in.
The light scares it away.
Who's out there?
What are your plans?

The Building

This building will be home for eight hours;
I work here after hours as a janitor.
The building some quarter mile long
Is vacant save one of us janitors.
It is quite a place to clean
But we have a system which works.
I clean imagining the people
Coming back to a clean office.
Also I enjoy the act of cleaning
Seeing dirt disappear or dust swept up.
The building is situated on a hill
A bit of rural life in the middle of an urban city
With oak trees strewn about
And squirrels, fox, and deer
I feel comfortable in my eight hour home
Living in this building toppling the hillside.

Sometime Job

Rolling out the trash, vacuuming the dust
I'm on my route
Of my sorta job.

I don't mind sweating at a job
I do so I can write.

I nudge my mind into a daydream
And I'm high into the clouds
Cut loose and fancy-free

Doing my wheeling-dealing job.

It's A Job

Today I hold a dustrag;
Yesterday it was a vacuum and a buffer.
It's my job.

Like an old bathroom towel
That's been used beyond its freshness,
I work on.

As if I'm a trampoline however
I bounce that idea straight away
Because I know the importance of working.

I work as though I'm conducting
A symphony to God.

My dustrag glides over furniture.
My vacuum whisks over the floor,
And my buffer sings over the tile.

Somewhere along the line I forgot I was working.

Waiting For A Bus (1)

Open eyes
And staring

Sunshine hot

Compensation
For the waiting

Is cool air
In the bus

When will it come?
Now? Later?
Today? Tomorrow?

I wait.
It's not so bad.

Sunshine hot
Gosh it's hot.

When the bus comes
There will be
Cool air.

I wait.

Waiting For The Bus (2)

Open eyes
And staring
Sunshine hot

Compensation
For waiting
Is cool air
In the bus

When will it come?
Now? Later?
Today? Tomorrow?

I wait.

It's not so bad.

Sunshine hot
Gosh it's hot.

When the bus comes
There will be cool air.

I wait.

Bus Window

Every ray I see through
The mud stained window
Is like fresh air.

The bus window, splashed
By some errant vehicle,
Has left me almost blind.

My stop comes.
I disembark.
Now I'm out there where
I couldn't see before.
The buildings: skyscrapers
Which are so tall
Are worth more than a life
To them.

It wasn't always that way.
The world's bigger than
I can manage.
I want to retreat
To my bus window.
Vision, now open,
Drinks intoxicating sights
Today. I'm not seeing
Rightly. Still the muddy
Window hangs before my eyes.

Dropped Off In Front Of A Tree

The bus pulled up short and dropped
Me in front of a tree today.
Sidestepping the wooden obstacle
I got to the sidewalk with little trouble.
It wasn't the day against me,
Just one of those things in the city.
Tossing it off with a laugh
I forgot all about the tree,
I forgot about the busride,
And remembered the laughter.

Untitled (2)

A moment of silence
Over Marquette Avenue
And business people
Buzz behind me
On the skyway
In downtown.
It's up to me now;
All of my dreams
Surface in a swirl
And then are quieted
By the view.
It's something two degrees
And something :39 minutes after
At the bank. I just can't see the sign.
Silent cars depart the city
And a few pedestrians last to
This hour.
A new day is happening to me.
I could be at Glacier Park
It's so still.
People leaving,
And me just starting.

My Saturday

I sit in the store -
Where I'm employed -
In a great armchair

And look at the neat
Stacks of clothes,
Linens, and books.

Somehow a store
All comes together
Out of miscellaneous goods,

And my mind
Comes together
From shifting experiences

Like a fine clock.

Sunday At Noon

The asphalt goes on forever in all directions
And I wait for the bus.
A sparrow glides down from the sky
Cocking his head back and forth expecting food.
Time stops... almost. The man in the T-shirt
Asks me for fifty cents.
I wait for the bus.
My Sunday best gives evidence
That I have come from church that morning.
I ponder the message delivered
And seek God's love.
I try to create images from this inner city corner
Amid the stubbornness and confusion antics of the street.
I see a gentle hope and ray of light.
The people are tough but they have their style.
Just don't look directly at them for they might
Not see you clearly.
I wait for the bus.
It is Sunday at noon.

[Poem that may be a fragment of a longer poem – 1]

Remorse, heavy like a hard clod of earth,
Or a wingless airplane, or a snake's birth,
Is a vehicle I can raise muster
To overcome wanton, reckless lust.
I bow my head for a moment of peace
And sin trails off and I sense release.

Philosophy

Serious At Life (1)

I blink at life
To see more clearly
Where and what it is.
I once stared straight
Into hell.
I now walk beside life.
Sometimes I gather my storm
And I go to the rooftops
Or higher.
Mostly, I think.
I play cautious ball
And I intertwine routine.

Serious At Life (2)

I blink at life
To see clearly
Where and what it is.
I once stared straight
Into the face of death,
I now walk beside life.
Sometimes I gather my storm
And I go to rooftops
Or higher.
Mostly, I think
I play cautious ball
And I intertwine routine.

Sweet Memory

The present is so ordinary, uneventful.
The future remains unpredictable.
I like to dwell in the loom of the past
Where my mind weaves contentment
Out of various threads, feelings,
Whatever has wrapped into me.
I am a hero in my memory
Imagining goodness in my motives.
My intentions were good, I say.
I have to see it that way.
Dreams stick to me
Like crayfish to creeks.
I am befuddled by life
But have dared big dreams.
The memory of dreams
Tastes sweet.
Cropping close to the heart
I gather steam to remember more.
I figure they add up to something
Which encourages me to go on.

[Poem that may be a fragment of a longer poem – 2]

Surpassing its measure now
I see the pine bowing lowly
To the onward growth of humankind.
Finally I see the pine and me as one-
A combination of what is and what is to become.

Untitled (3)

Taunting me overhead is a sparrow
In the trees across the yard.
He watches me with specks for eyes
Chirping in pride of his elevation
Brought by a gust of wind
One of a million sparrows in MN.
He is not so impressive to me
That I pay him much attention
I rather see myself in the tree
Looking on the world below
But no I am on the steps
And in human form
The bird is lesser than me
Yet holds his lofty pose
Make it no matter
The bird flies off and I go inside.

Wooded Walk

Winding through the woodlands and
Coming to an open space with a campfire,
Surrounded by nature by myself
Quite alone to do what I want.
Wanting to bare all my secrets
Wanting to know if I have any left.
Knowing the power of words unsaid
Keeping a vigil of silence
Only, harbouring them so long makes it difficult,
Needing to explode with life;
Return the trip back to people
Maybe no one will notice I was gone.

Fences

The bird hovers over the fence
As I reach for another thought
Like the bird, I was on top of a fence
Trying hard not to fall to either side.
But in my life, the fence moved
I had to constantly change to stay on top.
Yes, it got easier than it was
And life grew into higher fences
Which also made falling more treacherous;
I was careful, fences not walls
Where I could light on something temporal.
Then off to the next fence
And so on until I rested on a final fence;
Looking down I saw on one side an abyss
And on the other: Life!
I came down off the fence
And began living.

Sunset

Afternoon sunset offers to me enough
To cut the string and fly up.
The flaming sky,
And sun illustrating the image,
Bring me to nirvana-like state
Where I look down.
Time is so precious,
And love harder to find.
I am thankful for the
Window in the building.
Then just like it was never there,
The sun is gone.
Dutifully I work on
With a contagious memory of brilliant aftermath.

My Knives

My knives are Indian
The kind I learned on Franklin
Where young Red Men
Asked me for change, or love.
My tenderness was cut
by a surging urgency
To care for others
In greater need.
A doctor's knife
Or a young street knife?
I'll take the street knife
And make it rubber
It can bounce
Harmlessly off a cigarette billboard.

Lake Street

Cars roll along Lake Street
And a pink building says it all.
Young toughs in their cars -
Poor cars - not of the wealthy type.

They look for life and meaning
Along this narrow avenue

When the cosmos is so vast -
So like a young mind on Lake Street.

Winter Passed. Spring Jog

The clump of trees, a forest,
Compares to an individual tree
Like a smokey outpour.
I cannot imagine it all
The swamp is free of ice
Whereon wild geese nestled
Last season
and I asked,
'Are you O.K.?'
The highway is busy
And I try to cross
To continue my run
Amidst the trees, the forest.
Grace abides while temptation speaks
And the Spring answers
'Run like the dickens.'

There is an old stump
That could tell stories.

Something Found

Snow trumpets its way into life in winter days
I lay recovering from. Seeds have been long past
Harvested feeding the grain of my soul.
Now we are locked into battles of ice.
Travel is limited to necessary goals;
Frivolity finds itself indoors.
To get somewhere one must splice
Past and future to bridge today.

Spring

Fall winds blew once sending
Chills along my spine
Telling us that winter was coming.

Winter winds blew cold snow
And the harshness caused me
To go inward and tighten.

I waited for signs of Spring.

Spring came and blew warm winds
That set my spirit soaring so high.

I live in Spring now,
Etching out the limits of life.

It's In The Way

I would rather infer goodness -
Taking a path upward ...
Not particularly easier or shorter.

The green leaves
Are what I mean -
Here and gone,
Working to return.

Patience might turn the
Door knob -
A rubbing… soft and cuddly

Or perhaps it's a crocodile,
Steamed cappuccinos and speedboats.

Or glimpses... a barn swallow
Over the creek at dusk.

Telephone poles provide
A greater reach.

What is it then?
I'm sure it's the contagion
That cries out for more,
And that's when I'm
Very near to
Having it all.

Love

Untitled (4)

I want to discover you
With an earful
Of hope

That has drifted to you at night.
Everything that has left me
Wonders through my head
And heart like emptying pockets
Of poetry and pennies.

Young Death

Feather in the air at dawn
Drops near my feet,
Sent by an angel from heaven
To tell me something important.
'I have flown your world
To ignite the heavens
It's so beautiful here
Here's for your memory of me.'
I look down to pick up the feather
It's in my hand forever
I remember you so well
You left so early
I was sad to see you go.
Blossom where you are.

It Was You

The way you look at me it's like spikes
Going through my eyes.
No not you...
Someone that looked like you,
Who fell down, fell under, fell over.

The way you look at me it's like spikes
Going through my eyes.
No not you...
Someone who cared, someone who dared,
Someone with whom I shared.

The way you look at me it's like spikes
Going through my eyes.
No not you...
Someone I made love to.
It was you wasn't it?

Distant Dreamer

I caught your act
Just as you stepped
Towards something else
In another part of the country.
Couldn't quite see it
Fumbling, too high
And too difficult to attain
I made a decision
That has been broken
Now I turn against you
Because we couldn't be one
Anger is wasted
Tomorrow has come.

Dreaming Of Oceans Of Love

The tide is best at the beach
Where you can see it move.
I like your love coming to me
On a cool Autumn evening
Like a wave
Liberating my soul.
It's nice when it comes without asking
Because it's free.
It takes me out to sea
In living waters
Where I'd drown
Without you there.
The sea is many miles away
But I think about it.'
It's what I want to.
The sea is vast and magnificent.
Longing for oneness,
I await your love.

Lakes tickle,
Give me room without boundaries.

Personal

The Cut

My father cut himself
And I flinched.
He looked down at his hand
As if the blood was foreign to his body.
The cut wasn't bad
But it still chilled me
The way he reacted
Or did not react to pain.
I learned that toughness
Can be almost inhuman.
Sweat almost came off my brow
At seeing this.
I was flabbergasted
I didn't realize to feel was criminal.

Left Field

There is a saying for people who don't seem all there:
'They're out in left field'.
Well at the game tonight I felt like I was in left field
For a while when my brothers and father
Discussed the subtleties of a batter's stance
Or stats and names - the ins and outs of baseball.
I have to admit, 'I was in 'left field'.
But that's also where a lot of the game took place:
Three homers to left field (that won the game for the bad
guys).

What I did know was that my team had the worst record in
    baseball
And was up against the team that had the best.
It was all so predictable: the better team jumping to an early
    lead,
The pitcher handling a no-hitter through the fifth.

The home team showed a little spirit battling back...
Close enough to make it a game...
Close enough to make us stay and watch.

But for me the game really took place in left field
Those three homers... and me:
Lost among the new faces of baseball,
And the power of the visiting team.

The Beatles

At some irrational point in my life
I wanted to be famous.
Who knows, maybe that's why I'm up here now.
Anyway, I think that one rock band
Really worked hard to share their fame with everybody
And make the concept of fame readily available
That being the Beatles.
They reveled in their fame
And took on their audiences face-to-face.
Their fame was so accessible
That on one occasion I thought they said,
'Bruce Ario'.
In my grandiosity I thought
'My God, the Beatles are singing about me.'
What they really said I found out later
Was 'impresario.'

The Circus At 37

I drop my 37 year old frame
Nonchalantly into the stadium seat.
With the expectations of a nine year old,
I mumble something to my friends and wait.
Out walk the wide elephants
And the ladies in their spare costumes
Just like they were when I was nine,
When the circus had magic.
The tigers, the trick-playing dogs, everything,
It hasn't changed that much.
I remember the mobile homes I saw
When I came into the stadium
Where the performers eke out
Their frugal home life.
The homes were all laid out in rows
Just like the people in rows watching the circus.
I analyze it for a while
And realize, I can hardly wait to see it at 60.

My Virginity

Virginity can be thought of as like the seasons
Vital, full of zeal, full of grace
Yet long lasting, enduring, contemplative.

Virginity changes
Like the steel winter ice
To the smooth flow of summer.

Virginity harkens the spirit
As the fullness of spring
Or as fall like a dying emerald.

Virginity is born and reborn
Something like the seasons of the year
Running their courses and then again.

For Art's Sake

The distance between desire and reality
Is not that great if one is in the Christian pocket.
One is in the pocket
When dimensions are fixed
And one looks to the above,
And escapes the ground.
The pocket is like
The bag of water surrounding
A fetus in the womb.
Protecting against vexations to the spirit.
To have one's desire,
It's necessary to help others with theirs
Desires of a population
Are blended and interwoven.
I look out to see
Life ever rising.
Art is my desire
Which I come to as
A falling star
Wiggling through the night.

176

Taxi Driver

The taxi searched me out
And found me.
It was a more comfortable ride than the bus,
Which I had originally intended to take.
Furthermore, I would get there on time.
The taxi was the obvious choice.
The driver was in tune
To an undercurrent of political, spiritual truths.
I found this out by asking him
Where he was from.
He told me was from Ethiopia,
A war besieged country.
And we both talked about the ills of wars
Put on by old men for young men's expense.
The driver was nice but firm about his opinions;
I was tactical and questioning.
He got me where I was going on time,
Also, leaving me $10 poorer but still a little richer.

Reunion

Pine trees straight as clock hands
And crystal Lake Tahoe
Mark the condos where we group.

Our clan gathers,
Blood ties
Winding us around

This splendid setting.

We engage
In words which share
What time has relinquished.

Days, months, years,
Our paths have been stretched
Into different time zones – distant.

We touch today
In a reunion
Allowing time's magic to work

Us, roots of one.

'There's my cousin, aunt, father...
And isn't it beautiful weather .
You've got to catch me up on...'

Hasn't time lent itself
To bring us here,
The keeper,

Stopwatch of the real family.

Rendezvous With A Dog

I couldn't forget my pain
Over a knife fight
I had been in some years past.

Even my father couldn't console
The guilt, shame, and confusion
I felt.

So on a snow encrusted
Wintry day I ventured
Out feeling very empty.

The howl and bark of a dog
Would not let me go any
Deeper into hell.

Like Greek mythology
The dog guarded hell
And I tasted fear
But only so close.

Man's best friend must
Indeed be a dog
Because he pushed
Me upward

Back into the wintry day.

Patriotic Sinew

The lake water resembles gasoline
And it's too hot for ducks
Shading themselves like me under trees.

Everyone knows it's the Fourth of July
In the home of the gritty and brave.

At evening, elbows bump
Where we glue our vision to fireworks
Showing ourselves as citizens.

Somewhere deep we understand
Our liberty came hard and unevenly
So we grip what we can

Our minds wanting to burst like rockets
As we stick to our seats.

After it's over
People line out
On sidewalks where
It's thick for several blocks,

And we're tougher for it -
The flash and heat
Binding instead of consuming.

New Orleans By Plane

The tumbling clouds
Lifting our plane
Beyond, towards the sun

Into the sun
Over the
Checkered ground.

For several hours
We exist in our plane
On a different plane.

It is a fix
To get us
To New Orleans.

Then the clouds
Let us go
And we land and depart

As quickly as we came.

New Orleans

In little niches
Inside my hotel
Writing this poem.

Out from the streets
Out from the deadpan
Thick streets.

Yesterday's memory
Of the French Quarters'
Lazying pornography.

As soon as
Cajun chicken
Fried hits my mouth.

Like I ambulated
Through gates
Of the inner city.

And here I am writing.

Experimental

Week Ending

Lone day yields something
Blending the rest, blurring
All that grew together,
Dissipates like rain on the ground.
It surges and sways,
Kneeknocks me into a song
About relaxing and it
Soothes hinter undergirded
Powers to clouds above
Beyond and higher.
Rays through, together
Dropping me as I take time.
The birds are sparrows
The canteen gurgles
Past the river to the city
Of one people, underscores
My gravity.
No wrinkle, nothing gained.
Or lost.
It rolls off my watch
Into the ocean of the past.

Viewing The Pine (1)

The pine tree in my neighbor's yard
Towers over the blue roof.
It goes much higher than
My mild hopes for human welfare tonight.
Strong branches build up
To heights that are simply beyond my reach.
I give the tree my today
Because it existed yesterday.
Farther along I see myself growing
Tall and strong like the pine.
I see humanity grasping the height
Surpassing its measure now.
I see the pine bowing lowly
To the onward growth of humankind
Finally I see the pine and me as one –
A combination of what is and what is to become.

Viewing The Pine (2)

The pine tree in my neighbor's yard
Towers over the blue roof.
It goes much higher than
My mild hopes for human welfare tonight.
Strong branches build up
To heights that are simply beyond my reach.
I give the tree my today
Because it existed yesterday.
Farther along I see myself growing
Tall and strong like the pine.
I see humanity grasping the height

I Stumbled (1)

Stumbling no not falling
I only stumbled a little
Tripped up by problems
But I didn't fall
No, I remember I slipped
But I don't think anybody noticed
A small light downward movement
But not a complete fallout.

I Stumbled (2)

Stumbling, no not falling
I only stumbled a little
Tripped up by problems
But I didn't fall.
No, I remember I slipped
But I don't think anybody noticed,
A small light downward movement
But not a complete fallout.

Snowfall Night

I take time to pause
From my hurried dream
To watch the snowflakes
Brushed from the window.
Snow is good.
Brings moisture in the Spring
It is cold but wet
Must be from heaven.
I watch the snowflakes
And indifferently they land
Spoken language
Knows not such beauty.

Three

Important insignificant meaningful
Three periods, three innings
Three Gods in one.
The numeral 3
Bulges on the line
Like a stubborn trinity
Tricycles, triathlons, trilogies
Three-ring circuses, triplexes
and triple-feature Movies,
A number of important things -
Associated with the number three
Gives me time to think & 3 minutes to fry an egg.

Gone Away

Beyond a grasp I could contain,
A feeling of greatness and snap.
Too many roses on the bush
Now a single bud.

Looking Away

The rosebush was planted in the spring
quixotic flower protected by thorns.
In my narrowed garden I sing
replacing grief with a physical thing.
I am a dog without a tail, ox without horns;
the rosebush was planted in the spring.
I cared for it to watch its fling.
The flower is kind but my awkwardness scorns;
in my narrowed garden I sing.
A delicate plant with zing.
The flower has the courage to hear my mourns.
The rosebush was planted in the spring,
a gentle emotion pretty thing.
My heart remembers a child and forlorns,
in my narrowed garden I sing.
The flower stands to take me under its wing
over my body and feet with corns.
The rosebush was planted in the spring;
in my narrowed garden I sing.

Voyage

'Time waits for no one.' - Mick Jagger

Gentle friend and kind benefactor
I knew you before I began with my journey.

Holder of the ages
Stopping all things and allowing them all to happen.

My watch,
A calendar, or the bell tower chimes

Are ways we attempt to control.
You bring me forward: a summoning,

And a shutting down.
Hunger subsides and all ailments pass.

A mirror of the future
I hold you close

Tracing time
Like a razor over my beard,

The song of life.
The precious going forth.

Beat... Beat, Beat

Beat
The cry I hear
Of the city street.

Beat, beat
I'm down
At my brother's feet.

Beat, beat, beat
I'm homeless
And waging a war against...

Beat, beat,
...a life gone berserk
And grim.

Beat
My heart bounces down
The city street.

Beat, beat
No one to lay
Comfort...

Beat, beat, beat
...to eyes
swelled with...

Beat... beat, beat
...chaotic, formless,
Turmoil

Beat... Beat
day in and out.

Beat.

Publishable Arios – 265 poems

Philosophy

Snowy Impressions

The sky looks distant but clear
Thin ice that goes deeply above me
So I plant my feet and wait.

Coming down several hours
A day later and more like night
Except for the whiteness of my musings.

Light. Very light.
A feather would be heavier.
Men and women shoveling

Dust of a winter's landing.

Ice

Ice. The kind that makes you feel like a popsicle.
All over the streets. Manhandling the sidewalks.
Bitter. Cold.

The bus is way late
And I'm freezing
A hockey player out of the game.

I feel like a gerbil being tested in a lab
To see how much I can take
Or if I'll just solidify.

Reset. Somewhere a river flows and a bird sings.

Heat Can Be Had

Oh, we have heat. There is no doubt
When your face feels like a fry pan
You could cook eggs on.

Nonetheless, a stone skipping water
Has a life for a precious moment
And never forgets its feat

So don't despair over a little heat.
Just ask your congressman to vote green,
And let it rest. Better yet,

Take a trip to Alaska. Maybe become a citizen.

There's Always More

The one thing I can tell you, 'There's always more.'
It's a bold question, to ask for more
But good or bad, you will always get it.

Better than no never or not now
Strike presently when the kettle is on the fire.
Who'd want to be left holding the bag?

God has got your back
He wants actions to show your love
He wants you to know what you're getting into

Take out a loan. You can repay it.

Knowledge

A little knowledge is a dangerous thing
Causing false confidence in the face of the unknown
And when trouble comes, upheaval.

You can stay comfortable in your blindness
Behind yourself and in a glove
But you know, people see through you.

Do you like your image?
Do you care about your image?
Can you say a little more?

Will someone cry when you die?

Standards

I like people with standards
At one time it almost didn't matter what they were.
But now it does.

It's got to be standards that work for the good
Standards that say, 'Look what I've achieved.'
'I set a goal and accomplished it.'

Not so much, 'I've never done this or that.'
Where's the life to that?
You can't rest your laurels on what you haven't done.

Being able to forgive sins ranks high.

Standards?

Having standards won't help grief
Kings and queens suffer grief
It can affect one and all.

Certain measures can be taken
Stay active, journal, eat chocolate
Have a routine, sleep, eat healthy

But you can't work it out
Think it through
Or get over it.

You must make friends and bear it.

Fear Of Tears

Once considered a show of weakness
Now accepted as a sign of humanity
The times have definitely changed.

Driven to them is much different
Than a decision to let them flow
One is much better than the other.

To create them in someone else
Is a gift beyond measure
Ranking up with inspiring laughter.

Causing us all to be equals.

The Pole Is In The Way

Usually one can make the leap
Going side to side
Along with a snort of accomplishment.

No damage wreaks on heads
Of those caught up in dreams
Filled to capacity, fully replenished.

However, a sideways glance at
An object re-worn out of time
Can cause tribulation

Not to mention trials or songs to sing.

He Was Born To Overcome

Jesus was a lot of nots, and he was not merely God;
He was the pinnacle. Many people have tried to supplant
That Christmas hope, but it will not be done.

Imagine if it were: no joy, no miracles, no hope.
Jesus was a lot of nots, and he was not of giving up.
He started out as a king and remained that.

What if he hadn't? What if he settled down?
There would be no church, no saints, and no hymns.
Jesus was a lot of nots, because he was chosen,

Chosen to be the One to overcome and thus overrule all.

Is It A Step Or Is It A Hurdle?

Just ask Jesus what it took to roll back the rock
And walk after death.
Was it a slow or fast movement?

We may never know how to approach these things
And sometimes we move without knowing
How or why or even where.

It's a kind of blessing I guess in a lot of cases
Because we don't really want to know
And if we did

It would cause unlimited consternation.

Fighting With Words

If only they gave soldiers dictionaries rather than guns
And they marched into battle with diatribes.
We have lawyers. Why do we need bombs?

Words can slice better than any knife,
And language can bind better than handcuffs.
Is it too much to ask for intelligent warfare?

Why can't countries be held to their word?
Is it pandemic to mankind
To be suicidal?

Hasn't the time come to melt down the weapons?

Grabbin' It

It's the juice of a grape
Released when it's squeezed
By your teeth.

That pressure built under the skin
Pops out at your taste buds
And slides down your throat.

Life can be a grape sometimes,
A turn of events
Showering

Wetness at our senses.

It Comes Back To This

History rules but time offers
Money and gardens
Winnowing attention of the headlines

Treated like a migrant infant
Far away in front
Cool to the touch

In my chair for the duration
Opening closing all accounts
Drifting

Saved by the ringing phone.

Life's Follies

I like to return from the dead every now and then
To see what's really happening in our world
I slip on a pair of glasses offering a better view.

It's not that I like to be subject to pained
Looks of the misfortunes that are out there
Everywhere you turn you see heartache,

Nevertheless I owe it somehow
And maybe I can help through sympathy
To release a captive if only for a moment

And then I must decide: sleep or waking.

Took Up The Pen

Sometime ago or was it last week... today?
I decided to take up the pen
Which means a lot of things

But not money, spotlights, or big houses
More on the line of alleys, sunsets, and God,
And a touch of bleary eyes

Broken spirits, uplifted hearts, chaotic minds
And words. Is it just words?
Must be a combination of a lot

Don't forget the suffering part.

Bones

In the...
Trouble with the gravitational pull
Like they're yearning.

I've only broken one
Which is quite average.
They don't creak yet.

Surprising that they
All carry me
Where they do.

Now, my heart, that's different.

Hampered

I must have had my hands tied behind my back
Been blindfolded and standing on one leg
To not see it coming.

How did I think I could get away with it
Or pull the wool over everyone's eyes
And still walk in the light.

I had heard you must pay the piper
I just never thought there'd be so many musicians
Who went well beyond confessions

And got into heavy judgments.

Hedonism

Hedonism is a lot of fun
And quite the opposite of grieving
But one can easily lead to the other.

Sexual pleasure gratifies certain organs
But out of control it can end in insanity
Or worse.

Pleasure should be the pleasure of thoughts
And a desire to not hit below the belt
Noble desires for justice

And sleeping with a clear conscience.

Nocturnal

Nobody can really say what goes on in the evening.
Mystery remains mystery, and dark is dark.
Cool blend of one part night, the other part deep.

Crown me with a teardrop
And leave the radio on
Sit me in that old brown chair

I'll walk down the path of least resistance
And let it all hang out
Until the newspaper comes in the morning

Just don't let the Light forget how to shine.

Farmed Out

I never before noticed how straight the lights
Are down the street especially this night.
They almost blink like a landing strip

Or a guide to a pot of gold.
I'm going to stand here just a minute,
No time to get the camera.

If I was a little better
I'd walk a tightrope
Between them,

Or shuck and toss 'em in the combine.

Why I Walk Up The Down

A lot of people ask me about it
As if I was heading in a different
Direction from the start.

The difficulty comes in an answer
Which could give away my secret
Or send fallout to passersby.

If there was a straight line,
And that's all there was
Then we'd all be soldiers

Marching in someone else's war.

To And From

To a door behind which is
My mystery like an unfinished book
To be had in bite-sized mouthings,

From an unwinding staircase
With broken steps and a creaky handrail
As would be found in a mansion on the fringes of town,

I go to my future as a worn toy
Seeking newness, relief, and the pleasure
Of taping all my dreams

From my top to my bottom like a ladder.

Letting Go

Time comes around that grief must go
Walking and jumping and hollering
Over the wall and into the river.

But don't look back or they may catch you
If you take more than normal rest
Or worse, go back.

Set some new goals (find the goalposts again).
Get a haircut. Read the newspaper.
Reflect only so much.

Don't get boxed in.

Change

Please don't tell me that God doesn't change
Because that's mostly what God does.
It's Satan that is dead in the tracks.

The seasons, night and day, time
The very way humans age
Lakes freeze over and thaw

Opens possibilities like dice
Oh commitment still works
And the earth is a solid rock

But new is desirable and probable.

Freedom

The truth will make you free
Because the gatekeeper wants it that way
And all things point North.

Counterintuitive. Why not expedient lies?
Lies call you back like the phone.
They pop up at the worst times.

Truth is harder like the lumber your house is made from.
And it can even be fun like cotton candy
A joke between lovers.

No rule says it must be painful.

Trickery?

I learned the enemies' tricks
By going behind the lines
Far enough to learn their ways

But not too far to get stuck there.
Do the ends justify the means?
For myself I would have to say, yes.

Left breadcrumbs
Didn't lose the light
Put my faith in mankind

Time got me there; faith carried me home.

I've Walked Back

Excuse me for trying
But did I walk back?
Seems a beginning.

The pretense of the life I have
Pasted the glue
I didn't want to be a stuffed shirt

Snippets of what they said
Trying not to get stuck
You're so fine up there.

It's hell down here.

Close Quarters

I work in a fishbowl within a
Larger fishbowl
But our natural predators have been tamed.

So we enjoy our days
And the roles we play
Taking our cues and hooks

Treading the surface
Temporarily going under
Throwing out our lines

Basking under the fluorescent sun.

They're Fragments

Please don't bother.
You can see
It's just smidgens, a dust covering.

An opening door should not
Be concerning debris.
Close in, skip over it.

It's genre book
Pop tune
Mail returned to sender

A manhole cover hides more.

Past Currents

I still feel the river. The flow of my life
Is still there.
I've been waiting for the happy memories

And regrets make me stammer
Next to earth and hardball me
Into sullen streams

That cannot and will never satisfy
Like a smile or a butterscotch.
It would be a great gift

To never peer into that well again.

Perspective

Life is perspective and vice versa
Like leverages against a daunting reality
A view from the mountain top.

Most anything can be processed
And broken like a football field
Or music into notes.

It's the hardest to see yourself -
A creation or creator?
Half full or half empty?

Walk in my shoes and you tell me.

I Won The Toss

I have made decisions based on a coin toss
When I was younger
And reason was my enemy.

Now I look back
And wonder at the flippancy…
But not too long.

Freedom is a costlier choice these days
And I find myself
Compelled towards a welcomed stability

After knowing I could have lost the toss.

Creative Moments

I've regathered creative moments, a trove and a surprise
Much like when you have finally putted the ball into the hole
Or when you sit down with a classic novel.

My head spins upward so I must hold my seat
Running not running but drifting
Toward infinity or the far side of the room

So sure am I with no fear
Other than a push of time
Like I hold the answer

In notes on a page.

Gratuity

When I was a bartender I worked for tips
Sizable and otherwise
Coming in all directions - coinage, bills...

We all hoped there was something more
Definitely hoping because our wage
Was subsistence and our tastes unworldly.

They came bringing chunks of cash
And wheel barrows full of loot
Which caused us to splinter

Into economic units micromanaging our affairs.

Taking It Easy

Shouldn't have to work at it so hard
You are not saved through good works
Doesn't mean you have to be flip.

An occasional smile will suffice
Better still, get out for a walk
And when you're there, listen

Sounds indicate life which points a direction
Even newspapers opening on the bus
I always liked rock music

But not nearly as well as toast popping up.

Fishing Trip

A caravan of four men in two trucks
Emerges from the city at dusk
And reconvenes in a boat in the North Woods at dawn.

Idle chitchat, bickering, hints of foul-mouths...
But then the fish start coming
Who's going to catch the next one? Mine's bigger.

Around evening the friends
Are discussing old times.
A weekend packed with fishing

Serves to reacquaint, reassure, and resume.

Indications (1)

The highway crew spins yarn from their coffee as I
Pass down the vein back into Minneapolis.
Road construction riveted into my being like sound.

There will be a better road to travel - to get to know
Eventually. As it grows perpendicular to this city
There is a hint of growth suppressed only by material limits.

I'm really ageless the changes going on around me
Don't stop or settle because that's all there is.
And I don't mind really even though I can't keep up

I *try* with one more line... one more eyeful... another taste of it.

Indications (2)

The highway crew spins yarn from their coffee as I
Pass down the vein back into Minneapolis.
Road construction riveted into my being like sound.

There will be a better road to travel - to get to know
Eventually. As it grows perpendicular to this city
There is a hint of growth suppressed only by material limits.

I'm really ageless, the changes going on around me
Don't stop or settle because that's all there is.
And I don't mind really even though I can't keep up

I try with one more line... one more eyeful... another taste of it.

Housing

Wow, I'm lost on these superstructures
And the wind nips my face
Kissing ice.

The night time has brought lights
From within signaling a little life
Some chances of humanity.

The snowed trees support it
Like the would-be grass
And the walk is clear.

It's a damn building, O.K.?

Superstructure

It's built of a bigger, wider, and taller
Digression into space. I stand about
One window high, but I can see it,

Its bigger, wider, taller stance. I
Don't claim to outsize it.
My wits are my way up and out.

It looks quite odd next to a tree.
I would take a nap on its lawn,
And I know who made it,

I know its secret.

Can You Be?

Can you really be forgiven
Until someone stronger than you steps in
And breaks down your weakness?

Then you develop a strength of your own.
It might be nice to never be pierced,
But can that happen in this world?

Instead, when you are challenged,
See it as a blessing
A call to action

Seeking channels of recovery.

Pay Attention

Cars, vehicles, pirouette down the freeway
A dance through white-lined-dashes -.
The sight confirms my ideas of obedience

To some master plan played out
In this small display of traffic
Like a sign giving me the exit

I must take.
Where are they going?
And how will they arrive?

I will barely get there myself.

Rocks And Stars

Get that stone out of your pocket
And see if you can skip it on the river.
You're too young to be a rock.

Befuddle someone else's mind
With a piece of pie
Or a glimpse of a star whether

Human or celestial.
Your scope isn't a mouthwash
Because you can chart a bigger question

And you can skip off the river to the sky.

A White Desert-Oasis

I was stepping on
Serving the inner drive
To a walk-a-thon to pay for existence.

But the weather is snowy
And the trail's been covered over
Blinked to come to.

Encounters with a type of contagion
Or a flirtation with the elements
A nonchalance of vision

Equaling each other.

Tidings

We set sail at high tide
When you could get out to sea
Easily through the varying currents.

Our ship was a tightrope
Bouncing on waves, a yo-yo
Barely room for us.

Then we stayed in it many days
Seasick, hungry, and boxed in
Until we spotted destiny

A shoreline just coming up.

Leaves In My Mind

Don't let them touch your head
Signal showing what's to come.
Is that a leaf or a snowflake

Blowing above the street?
So happy on their way out
It's a relief letting go.

The trees however will soon be lonely
No leaves attached to give hue.
But they'll be back

The purveyors of a merry-go-round.

Tally Two

We swindle each other
Below. Above we are saints in a glove
Of kindness. Couldn't we catch

The train out? My body numbs
In refrigeration, a case
Of following a race

To its core. Would you
Hit me? Would you
Come along and feed

On the breadcrumbs we laid down?

Suppressing Mutiny

Light from a single focus enters the heart
Finding me like a needle
Possibilities of much but one path.

Every stray glance a blow
Bringing me to the brink
Of no return.

But I must return. Again and again.
Becoming comfortable with being uncomfortable
Leaning on resolve, a post

Looking not so much up or down - sideways

Waltz In Waltz Out

Sometimes you hardly know you've been there
Except you've got a receipt
And there's a chunk of your watch gone.

But down the road you remember
Could be the fragrance that gives it away
And you wonder if it matters.

There are no pictures, no tape recordings
You're sure no one will know
But you know better

The long hard night has just begun.

Tic Tac Tock

But you made an uncircular motion
I wouldn't have been more buried
If I was looking for tree roots.

And that's what I found: antigravity.
I was sprung like a spring
Air shoes

When it doesn't matter
Then I'll know
Figments

Please pertain this to something good.

It's A Clock

Giant mounds of paper dissolve
Under the work I seemingly
Sweat over.

The image is a pendulum
Or a tennis player
Training for rhythm.

It may mean a lot to someone
But I'm content when the stack diminishes
And I could go back to before

When things were not allotted out.

Timer

Time winds through my mind
As a narrow thread of being.
It's faint like wind.

I feel as if I'm escaping the timer
Because of a sensation of life
Which defies me to define.

The timer in my soul ticks ad infinitum
An eternal measure
Beyond all comprehension

As though the timer is actually perfunctory.

In And Out

I've been there, done this, done that,
And sometimes I laugh about it
Whether right or wrong.

Laughter not chosen but forced
Is wanton like a shooting star
Fading into dark skies.

I've been out of laughter
A car run out of gas
A tree stump all that's left of nature.

So in and out of laughter like water and sand.

The Way

People have told me that beauty
Fades with age
A sun settling into a moon.

No. I've seen beauty grow
Like a picture at a drive-in movie
Into a work of art in a museum.

Beauty is the alpha and omega,
A match to a bonfire,
Ignition to a rocket,

And a thought to a poem.

When Rust Is Cleansed

All you really got to do is use elbow grease
A strong cleanser goes a long way
And a piece of terry cloth works fine.

My co-worker told me
He cleaned his bumper with Coke
But I like a good industrial acidic.

After a couple of hours of work
You make progress on the shine
And you get your surface back

However, you will never have your original.

Non-Communicated

It was too hard to communicate
What I needed to say.
And that's coming from a writer.

At the time there wasn't enough time.
Now there's been too much time
It's become harder.

I'm not a Nike 'Just Do It' commercial
It could never be perfect
And take you to the top.

I'm kind of glad it never was.

She Was Wrong

I had the wrong girl, wrong place, wrong time.
Should have been an easy decision
But it took four decades to resolve.

That's OK. Some people never work it out.
At least I can enjoy my senior years
In the bliss of knowing the truth.

My mother really gave me the freedom
On her deathbed that night:
'I hope it was worth it,' she said.

Survival is a great thing when it works out.

Slumming

When your heart is in your shoe
After you've taken the plunge to find someone new
You can't help jumping a beat when you do.

Time spent wandering up and down
Going through the motions throughout the town
It's been a circle game round and round.

To think you've finally found her
When she treats you like a sir
And she makes your heart purr

Then you know you've got her tear.

I Mean No Offense

The woman approached me on the street,
And she started out by saying,
'I mean no offense.'

None taken. I could see her desperation
So how could I be offended by her request for money?
The disappointing thing is I didn't give her any.

But offended? No. Not hardly.
I mean there's plenty to be offended about.
How about the fact she needs to beg for her needs?

To the woman: how about we both be offended?

Where Have All The Smiles Gone?

I'm borrowing an idea from a sixties song
And a lament as old as humans.
Why all the tense retinas?

Or faces as straight as buildings?
If it wasn't so peculiar to be having fun
We might truly rejoice in bliss

Of a gift most precious.
What holds us in our states
Of corporate stiffness

And makes our mouths curve downward?

We Were In Only A Minute

We didn't steal it or anything
If I remember right there were no keys
If there had been, who knows?

His fault for leaving it open.
I was trying to impress her
Too drunk to know better.

I know it wouldn't look good on the resume
But nobody saw us.
So why am I telling you now?

Confession can be a good thing.

Both

I'm not quite sure how it ended up like this,
But I'm in the situation that it's both.
Both of us, both of them, both of whatever.

It took two to make it happen this way,
And it's gonna take two to get out alive.
A couple of things I want to say:

A knot is tied with two ends of a string
And there is a sun and a moon
Even Christ had a mother

Walk beside me if you want to be near.

We Won't Then

You said it offended you when we did
So we stopped doing it for your sake
Because we thought you were right to say so.

And we didn't want to do it anymore anyway
We just had grown too far apart
Even a bridge couldn't work.

And so to save face we split
Down the middle in the heart
Where it hurts like a grenade

Nonetheless, we will heal, at least I will.

When It's Endless

Going under, drowning in an ocean
In the middle, no shore
Zapped, targeted, and isolated

A dive into yourself
With lead weights around your arms
Heavy, too heavy, very heavy

Nothing up only down, down
Fading lights out of reach
Graceless tired mire

Sinking, trying to swim, sinking.

His Time

Not thinking I'd ever make it
Waiting like for an Italian train
A Godot for my life.

Suppositions offered freely to me
Only a few containing any weight
Popcorn at a movie

An attempt made to be above it
Hot air balloon?
Only then

Realizing the waiting is over.

Love Of Literature

Words are probably the closest
People can come to divinity
Or to eternal damnation.

It all depends on intent
And the way they're arranged,
Which is especially true of literature.

A master is able to make words sing
Like a symphony
Or paint pictures with stories

That summon up our deepest breath.

Good Girl Bad Girl

It gets kind of confusing because
Each type serves their purposes
At different times.

And maybe that's the problem
When we can't see
That all people are some of each.

Good? Bad?
Who am I to judge?
Girls are girls, period.

Now, a woman. That's a different question.

Why Can't You Control Your Motorcycles?

I want freedom too,
But when did freedom become
Six men raping one woman?

You thought you were driving your bikes in the sun.
Instead you drove your motorcycles straight between her legs.
I want to see the look on her face.

Why couldn't you control your motorcycles?
You went too far beyond the bend.
You sailed right into moonrock in the Vatican.

Now she will park your bikes.

She's Got A Right To Say, 'No'

People have a right to draw a line
In the sand like my preacher
Said he'd do about abortion.

He was all about pro-choice
And women need rights
To include saying, 'No'.

They are not required to say, 'Yes'
To any wild question from the stratosphere.
Sometimes 'No' works.

And they don't need me to tell them that.

Won't Take A No

I don't think God intended us to accept a 'No'.
Everything about God is a 'Yes'.
Affirming, reassuring, positive

In gentle measures mostly
Like leaves clinging to the trees in the wind
Or rivers winding out their ways through the earth.

We agree to all terms in all places
As long as it has the ring of truth
And as long as the alternative is 'No'.

Then bring on the nodding heads and open eyes.

Rejection (1)

There's only one rejection that's permanent
And I don't believe that is either.
Don't lose course or hang your head

Time will heal that wound
And there'll be a ship on the horizon
God will let out some line, then pull you in.

Pay no matter that what people saw in you
Has been rejected
If it was worthwhile, it's still there.

Just never, ever reject yourself.

226

Rejection (2)

Rejection causes immediate grief
Because you wanted something
You couldn't have.

Your apple cart is toppled
Your dime misspent
Your one chance vanished

Before you nothing
It's all behind now
Just can't quite realize it

You must just take steps now.

When It Hits

When grief first hits you know right away
There's no up or under or escape
You're in for a long ride.

Nothing anyone can say takes it away
It's a solo journey
That kind words lessen the avalanche

But cannot heal only comfort
Like a band aid
For a wound like the Grand Canyon.

Sit back, take it slow, keep moving.

Sensitive

You can take a stance that grief is sensitive
A ring on her finger
A bottle of lemon sparkling water

You can say almost anything about grief
But not everything said is true
One thing it moves in stages

Sinking into the bottomless void
Finding the bottom
Climbing out of the hole

Keeping what you learned under your hat.

Grief Is Love

Incredible grief comes from incredible love
When there is a loss and a break
From that which you were so attached.

The abyss is filled by wanton emotion
And uncontrollable irreconcilable turbulence
Loneliness like a golf ball.

I can't come up to the surface
Which is out of my reach
And beyond my means.

I'm drowning in a type of love: lost love.

The Goodness Of Grief

Just as people need water and food
Nothing cleanses the soul like righteous grief
Not the despairing type but turnaround grief.

The kind that draws you to heaven
In awe of your vast limitations
And your penchant for balm

That heals fractured egos
And makes you whole
Ready for the fight

And sensitive to the mysteries behind masks.

Can I Afford It?

Can I afford to have all this grief?
What if the load is too much?
Where will I be if I fall?

You find yourself at church
Where people know your grief
But also your joys.

So you shoot for the middle
A little sorrow over the situation
And laughter over yourself

So that's how they meet on any given night.

Become Yourself

Hardly an ending, it's on
For as long as we know.
Do something like a reply.

Handed down like jeans
From an older brother
I got life.

So I extrapolated a bit.
It's hardly a crime,
Where someone wanting time

To pinch me into their sight.

Toehold

Desperate search for a rock
It's nothing but quicksand you find
But you must think, think like a book.

At first it seems obvious
Something you've been told all your life:
Jesus died on a cross for your sins.

What does that have to do with me?
It's for everyone freely offered
Something to let go for.

Now you're free to think what you want.

You'll Only Hafta Say You're Sorry

You can try to be discreet and hide,
But they'll ferret you out
And haul you in.

So don't do it
Stop and think
Put a lid on it

You'll be happy in the morning
That you resisted
That you didn't cave in

Think of the money you'll save.

I Surmise What Happened

I don't know for a fact but I can guess,
It's just a matter of adding two plus two
An open and shut case.

I won't go into detail or anything
To tell you what I figured out
By way of deduction.

You did it; both you and I know.
Who do you think you're dealing with?
I'm not going to bust you for that.

Just sign an affidavit and send it to me in the mail.

A Moment of Clarity

Punctured my weakened mind
A song that let me into myself
Simple, yes, like tic-tac-toe

Or more magical than a cloud
When looking too close
Something ungraspable

But substantial light
Enough that someone noticed
Besides me

And who knows who else.

Subtlest

Almost passing unnoticed like a needle
Except for the poke
That comes at the strangest time.

Poison drains along with the good
But not from memory
You can see them both if you look hard

And you wonder if you took it
Back into your system.
You want to distinguish between them.

It takes the subtlest view of the world.

Not Sure How To Play It

Your deaths were a game-changer
And I know you didn't want it that way
But fact is fact.

Not quite sure what to do
Feel like an amputee.
The loss is stunning.

Me and the Beatitudes cover my days
And I try to get a grip
But the walls seems so blank

And tomorrow an eternity.

Evil

If you have your experiences in life
You're going to encounter evil
And what are you going to do about it?

You need to understand that evil
In and of itself is not the problem.
It's putting evil in gear

And taking action in a bad way
That makes evil have consequence
And have results that are hard to fathom.

Evil alone - nothing. Evil in action - destruction.

Japan

Warrior nation neglecting charm
In favor of money, victory, and achievement
Never slow at the gate.

Crowded onto a shoe shaped sized island
You seem to grow outward
Toward the eye away from sound.

Puncture my sun and moon
Until I can't tell I'm not you
Or that you stood for more than

Yen around a chain - encourage me.

The Bull

Behind the gate, rider on my back
Tension high like a drum
I know what I'll do when I get over

To the other side of the fence.
I'll destroy him
Into little pieces

Run him around like a cyclone
Put him in a blender and spin it
Erupt this volcano

Walk him off a plank.

Accidentally

'The asphalt gets slippery
after the crew washes the streets.
But what were you doing racing him anyway?'

Cracked windshield, bump like an egg
I'm not sure where I was or am anymore.
Doesn't mean the world's come to an end.

It's just been turned upside down or something.
I was just trying to...
'You really didn't know did you?'

Well, I guess I never expected...

Progeny

At dinner tonight with your progeny
I reflected and ate
Asked questions and drank

On and to a situation impossible
Without your union
Now held in the sky above

Or some other unknown sanctuary
While we still nibble and sip
Off plates and from cups

That belong to us for a second.

The Best

It was something too good to believe
Yet, it fit like a glove,
A wonderment and a fact.

Now I'm not saying
It would be proven in court
At least not as we know them today,

It's just that
If you look long enough
Then you will know

What he meant when he indicated I was the best.

Tugging

Sweet chain of events which could have
Blocked my dreams has dropped
Blossoms to my mind

Opened to a tumble
Of emotion that submerged
Until I came out the other side.

It left me seeking brightness
Sturdier footsteps
Sequential

Until I wanted galaxies.

Peace Of Nations

When humanity tires
Choosing to elevate the soul
From itself gone awry,

Then we might see purpose,
The cold clang of the bell
Mourning our lost ways,

The vacant lots
Of people who have moved out.
Into, we go into it

With wide steps.

I Can See The Trees Now

They have changed in my eyes
No longer like a museum
More part of nature.

And I am separate from them
Which is a source of grief
But also relief.

They have met their limit in my soul
I have seen them in their ultimate glory
And I just can't go higher.

Beauty has its limits

Over The Fence

So much is permanent like a fence
I considered it a lost cause
Thought I would be peering over jealously forever.

But that's all in the past now.
Climbed night and day
To get over the fence

Just to get to the pasture
Where the grass is greener – exponentially,
By a margin of 1 to 50.

Will take time just to adjust a bit.

Second Chance

The jump over the fence was a second chance
Coming up short the first time
And face-to-face with a thick and opaque fence.

Could have given up hope right then and there
But a light led me onward
Then I saw stairs and moved up them

Until I got a grip on the top
Pulling myself up and over
Jumping to the ground

Standing in a land open as an ocean.

The Past Goes Way Back

I remember being fenced in not able
To see over as if barb-wire
Kept me contained and limited.

Then I discovered music
Or rather that which I'd known
Took on new dimensions.

And soon I could look over
The room that I found myself in
And feel a little important

As though the fence had no meaning.

Personal

The Circumference Of A Square Room

Sitting pensively aware
Of the four corners
This mailroom is bounded

By, I realize
That life is really
Circular and unbounded

Through things like mail
Traveling the globe
And going to areas

Around the circumference of the world.

Visits

Flick, flick. Tang, ting. The mail finds its way
To the gray metal cubby hole.
It goes to names I have no face for,

Except a few who make visits.
Especially the one who tells us the stories
About her children, their trials and activities.

It's nice to give mail to someone you know.
Even junk mail takes on meaning.
When she's leaving there is always just

One more thing to say, one last story.

Forward

How'd you do it?
Kept me moving forward
Like a stamp

Even when I was addressee comatose.
Oh, there'd be others to take credit
And maybe some could

But it's undeniable
That you had me date-stamped
Somewhere off in the future

When my letter was undelivered.

Escaping Through Fiction

I discovered fiction
Could be that great trip
To the beyond

When I had become bent
From drinking and drugs
And all that mess.

A good story can put me
Into a series of oohs
All the way into the night.

It's my painless, airy flight.

Doesn't It Happen That Way?

I twist on the shower that turns into a toothbrush
Running my mouth through as I drift into breakfast
And arrive at work like a bus.

Then things happen so much that I wish
I could but I can't afford to so
Stumbling and growing fonder of the

Time which waltzes a box step
Of my mind into a figment transposed
On the computer until I'm off for the day.

Man, the chances God takes!

Bouncing Off Blondes

I don't mean to sound disrespectful;
It's more of a phenomenon
Than anything negative.

I have to explain that in a city like Minneapolis
Blondes come bouncing down the streets
Like spring flowers in park gardens.

I just can't understand the whole person -
But blonde hair is something I can handle
Because of the beauty and confidence

Like a winner's walk after the race.

Odometer

Jogging by at a safe speed
Still not knowing any one place
Too much.

Movement prohibits
That which would cling.
Measurable distances covered

Like all that I'm missing.
What's that blossom?
How cold is the water in the lake?

Can't we stop for some coffee?

The Off-Season

No need to exert myself now
Because the marathon is months away.
I am in the off-season

When runs untimed
Turn into walks,
And my steps come closer to each other.

This coming summer I will train harder
But for now, the winter sights
Capture me in my slower pace –

Substituting joy of vision for sweat while training.

Justice

'Justice is the answer,'
I told my professor
In my first class at law school.

Justice is like the whipped cream
On French silk pie,
Or the fork you eat it with.

The world cries out
For justice -
Just a piece

To get your mouth onto, small meal.

Why I Wait For Justice

When I was in law school, justice was a
Bandied around idea much
Like a tennis ball rallied on the court.

I never felt I found justice there though.
Perhaps it was because I could not wait.
I'm almost certain some law students

Believed in the virtue of justice
And would even extend themselves
In an effort to bring it forth.

That's why I'm waiting. Not giving up; just waiting.

Playing By The Rules

In law school it was impressed upon my mind
That to succeed one must play by the rules.
Every day I relearn this platitude.

But when I'm not playing the game
There are no rules to break
I simply am.

So what I'm saying is
I'll play your game by your rules
But when it's no longer your game

Then I'll thank you to leave me alone.

I'm A Democrat (1)

The subtle ways I distrust Republicans
Even though I'll work across the aisle
And strive to be fair.

But mostly I distrust Republicans
Not that they're inherently bad
I just feel they're misguided.

Dirty tricks, innuendo, false claims
It's all so tiring and time consuming
Like I didn't have anything better to do

Then try to instill reason in an iceberg.

The New Year

The calendar flipped over to '96
And I steadied and got ready
For a New Year.

It is the time to make plans
Assess the past
A time of beginnings and chopped off endings.

A circular game
That the solar system
Plays out in the heavens,

Becomes my little challenge.

Focusing On The Colors Of Summer

Blue river, bluer lakes, and bluest skies
Lush greens of leaves and the tall grass
Rainbows of flowers gardened in yards and parks

I might walk down a brown road in the country
Next to white fences
Sizing up red barns

In the city I walk down gray streets
Watching yellow, black, red, white, and brown
People circling

My summer of color.

Dusk At Sunset

The evening sun kisses the sky goodnight
With a farewell of rose colored brilliance.
The bus I'm riding heads east away from the display

So I must look over my shoulder
And back towards the West
As I think about the earth rotating.

The darkness moves in over the streetlights
Suspended somewhere between here and the moon
While children nervously ride their bikes home.

It's Friday night and another week passes.

Vacation

I closed doors to the working week -
Time to take that vacation:
Relax, unwind, rest, and write.

Even my jogging routine spun out
By way of a twisted ankle.
So there was nothing

To do. Waking up late,
Eating out in coffee houses,
Wandering streets and skyways,

The settling in to aimless hours.

The Cafeteria In The Morning

The yellow lights –
Brighter than the moon
Softer than the sun

Dim my way
Packaging ideas
While the flowered tables

Where I rest
To gather sustenance
All make together

For a quiet time of review.

I've Arrived

Sizing up the avenue
I confidently stroll
Down sidewalks

Past corners
And through lights
Until I come

To the building
Where I work
Just in time to start.

A glance at my watch tells me I'm even early.

In The Store Alone

Because my job is after-hours
No one is left around
And I'm there alone.

I cleaned the ramp
And I cleaned the downstairs
You can accomplish a lot by yourself.

The eeriness of it all
Can be had by keeping on task
And not giving into wild imaginations.

Thus the store gets ready for others.

Customer Service

When I can be of assistance
When there is someone who needs me
When I can help

Then I feel wanted
Then time has been well spent
Then I'm complete

And a feeling of warmth comes over me
And I feel a little higher
And feelings are joyful

But only if the person receives what I'm giving.

Cleaning The Store

The cleaning vacuum sings along the carpet
And I am wheeling along
Almost doing nothing.

Each stroke
A spot of clean
And I move along

Until I'm done
And all of the dirt
Is trapped in my vacuum bag

And I've barely done a thing.

Utility Man

Sounds of vacuuming, the quick slice of the cardboard box
Piled in a cart for recycling, water rinsing coffee cups,
Testing a lamp for saleability

Putting price tags on hard goods,
Toting bags to the basement,
And garbage cans to the dumpster

Eating on the run, answering the phone,
And sweeping the back hall,
Getting change for the cashier and selling,

My list of jobs as manager of a thrift store.

Thrift Store

You were like the hanger oscillating
On the rack before I picked you from your perch
And drew out the dress you were wearing.

Then you became a box.
Something like a jewelry box
But full of songs and whispers.

Finally you were furniture to
Move around and feel at home.
However, you never became a household.

You remained far more fleeting.

Heading Towards Home

I walk out of the store after work
Up a ten foot wide ramp
Onto a six foot wide sidewalk.

This takes me up to the small park
Where the path winds through
Until I come to pass between two buildings

And get on the single avenue of my home.
I put the key in the security door,
And then into my door and into my one bedroom condo.

What a narrow life I lead now that you're gone.

Calls At Night

A green mop surfaces the bucket.
A buffer slides over a shiny floor.
The janitor thinks about other things.

The fire in the voice of the grey panther
Who is politicking, working...
Is a deep resonance.

What would a grey panther have to do
With a sometime janitor?
How could they ever get together?

In phone calls at night.

To Sing A Song Of Clean

My song skips through my hand to my dustrag.
Over the woodwork it sings
Melodies of cleanliness.

It's an idea I learned at
Home and church
And brought with me to work.

I negotiate dirt and dust
In circular motions of the hand
Like a conductor

Zip, pad, hum, sing, smoothing out the dirt.

Dust Had Settled

Dust had settled on the office furniture,
Various electronic equipment,
And books.

It's not from non-use but high-use,
And it was a quiet moment in the morning
When I took out the wand.

Doing a quick flick with my hand
Dust particles were banished to the air
Sent on the run

Probably to resettle some other time.

While I Cover The Floor (Thoughts Of A Janitor)

Another senseless murder,
Yet, another baby being born.
I sweep the floor.

Five and a half billion people as my neighbor,
And many as my friend.
I mop the floor.

The sun sets;
A crescent moon wanes in the darkness.
I buff the floor.

Expectations of a clean floor.

The Bathroom Chronicles

I find myself polishing chrome sinks in a building
Where prisoners have ceramic floors
And white bars where they hide all day.

It's a holding cell and I'm a janitor.
As I match my rag to the toilet
I feel a duty binding my hand.

The people in the cell
Will detect my work -
The cleanliness.

It's enough.

Garbage Out

Minimal job on the receiving end of things
A task I do not cherish overall
Which buries my heart so it can't sing.

Groping my cart I wheel through the halls
Picking up the day's haul
Making a pile of all of it by the wall.

One redeeming factor, one bright spot
Is knowing that I'm giving them all a new calling
To work some more until they've got

More trash tomorrow I'll get from their stall.

Climbing Stairs

Skipping every other like Jimbo
The tall lanky guy
From the other crew

I walk up the building.
It's like a life that I climb
To reach heaven.

With a broom or towel
Or with deep prayer,
I've learned to

Take the direct way up.

30 Years

I suppose what it will be
Like when I started those years
As a sophomore something, something.

How many staircases have I climbed
To be where I can remember
Running down them to be first in the lunchroom.

Time has ticked or has it rendered
Me a more complete picture,
And I head to my reunion

A head shorter but leg up.

Jogging At 39

The edge of night settles
Over my head and my legs go
Thumpity, thump.

All around the sidewalk
On both sides
The foliage has grown in.

While every breath is a heavy one,
They're all triumphs
With a bit of glory written into it.

The body goes along with what the soul wills.

Getting On With Age

At age 30 I felt a sharp pain in my ego.
The stitches in an old pair of jeans
Or an apple sliced apart to its core.

By now at 41 I keep a journal
Which goes into detail about my journey
Into this forward push of the years.

And I dig deep
Not willing to go quickly like lightning.
And there is relief

In walls climbed, walls removed.

In The Bushes

I always tried to take them out to the bushes
At high school keggers or beer parties
Not knowing any better.

Change the scene forward five decades:
I haven't had sex for 30 years.
There has to be a happy medium.

Somewhere with soft music
A nice meal
A cozy room

The right one.

Her Nylons

I've always liked the look of nylons
On women as they wisked down the sidewalk
Showing off their most beautiful legs.

I could almost be a crossdresser
Wearing nylons at home
To feel their silkiness next to my skin.

But I believe I will find a woman someday
Who greets me at the door at night
Wearing nothing but sheer stockings

And an invitation to touch.

The Nature Look (1)

The bend of the willow tree is very erotic
Especially in the wind as today
I watch like a voyeur

Or, skip over the ice on skates
A boy with dreams
The opposite of grasping

Where you can hear the song
Birds calling me?
But from my window

I am a foreigner anxious over deportation.

Straight Line

I don't desire a straight line to your heart
Exit off the freeway
Gravel roads offer a better chance

To really see the country
Feel the trees
And hear the sky

Any lummox can steal your soul
Unless you've bound it to infinity
So walk

Untroubled like the lake purring at the shore.

I Called Her

When I got the message I called
And felt my heart
Shaped by the sound of her voice.

Tumbling with words
Cautiously timing
And waiting for my turn

We go out together
To the crook of a tree
Peering, peering, peering

So sad to say goodbye.

Lofting It Into Friendship

I may have had designs, I don't really know.
It's all unimportant now
Because she just wants to be friends.

I've heard the words before -
The sound of a yellow light blinking
Its warning.

Friendship, though, that's not bad.
It could have taken worse turns.
I could be thankful.

Friends is where it ends.

Music Can Cure

I like to cue up a good blues record
Lay down on the couch
And commiserate with myself.

As I lie there I often weep
For no reason at all
Other than catharsis

And I remember her
How our lives intertwined
And it makes me sad

To reach out and she's not there.

Ice Cream

I remembered when Dad
Would eat half a gallon
Of ice cream in one sitting.

I'm not trying to make excuses
Or say that I'm just
Following Dad's example,

But I polished off
A pretty good helping
Of chocolate ice cream this evening.

I know I shouldn't have.

Didn't Say Anything

Dad, I still remember your wince
When I'd say something wrong
About somebody.

Mom, I can remember
How you'd candy-coat
Descriptions of others.

Mostly I remembered
To watch my words about others
Forgetting sometimes admittedly.

But with her, I didn't say anything.

Was It Worth It?

Your big question to me, Mom,
And if I know what we're talking about,
Then no, the price was greater than the value.

But if it's meant to ask, would I do it again,
I'd have to answer yes
Simply because cost should not be an object

In the realm of the soul.
And when you start out on a trip
You should finish it

And hoping, God hoping, you will return.

Grieving For Mom

I still think about when she left that night
What was she trying to tell me?
I can only ponder that

But I can make some good guesses.
Beyond the superficial, she loved me
Was that she really loved me.

And I know she was trying to say goodbye
But there was something more
Almost the keys to the city or something

Maybe she was thinking about my writings.

Replacing It

There was a book called 'Who Moved My Cheese?'
And I'm sure mine's moved several time zones,
Not to mention a lot of other stuff.

So I'm replacing it.
A new engine will be put in shortly
And a new roof too.

I'll be going new places,
Have a new address book,
Get a new payment plan.

Take off that lasso around my neck so I can breathe.

I Glow At The Possibilities

They are saying I can recover from mental illness.
While most of the time I didn't even think I was.
It was always their word.

Now it doesn't hardly matter
What I'm called
It's more who I am.

To be more definitive
I'd say I accept life
And I don't do

Those obnoxious spins.

In For The Duration

The hit on the head in a car accident
Was mismatched by a visit from heaven
Like mice and horses.

I won't wonder one without the other;
That's how it happened
Turbulence and tranquility.

I'll take the second and leave the first
Choice between heaven and hell
When the only wager required

Comes from opening your mind.

Grief Had Me Down

Sinking muddy quagmire of a fix
So encompassing that even friends
Couldn't outlast.

No solution occurred to me
Running like a fool
Away, away, away.

Then I came face-to-face with Christ
And knew it was my last chance
And I felt such release

Freeing, really freeing, if just for a moment.

It's Lent

Ash Wednesday tonight like a door
Swung open and a challenge
To wrestle with myself

With the purpose of goodness
Coming through insight
And thoughts now I don't know.

But I do know that something is out there
Calling me
I must put one foot out then the other

Until I meet a destiny I never will.

When You Figure It Out

When you finally figure that you've just been chasing sin
Your whole life and you wonder if that's all there is
And you're shown a new way by way of the Cross.

Or did you have it right from the start
And you were living without sin
Eventually coming face-to-face with ultimate sin

And you know you didn't want that
But what did that make you, Christ?
And you knew you had to turn to Him

And yes you still sinned, but you were trying to get over it.

Just A Prayer

Lord, when you sent your angel
I didn't really know what to make of it,
The situation of being in the presence of Christ.

But I knew it was good
So I tried to spread the Word
And it's been an interesting 40 years.

I've never regretted but stumbled a lot
My way since then
But never let go

Just become a little seasoned.

I'm His

Decision's been made and handed down
My angel claimed me for Him
Led me straight to the cross.

No way I could say no or not yet
I was sealed like a letter
After I had run through the thicket

And done my damnedest not to deserve Him
He was out front of me
A white light moving towards the heavens

Me below uprooted, turned around, praying.

Staring At Sunday

Sunday's my best day which is free
From protocol of time, work, and money.
It's like a season combined of the

Best reasons to spend life in peace
Because there exists no
Stress, pain, or grief.

The tulip lips of a Sunday afternoon
Caress my mind
Like a bulb from a dim light

Throwing out just enough vision from God.

The Word Of God

The heads of the congregation are all so straight
As if they say I don't want to miss an intonation,
Or one syllable of the message by the minister.

The narrow aisle is empty save a memory
Of the people who came in minutes ago, now seated
In hard wooden pews whose straightness uplifts

My weary body this Sunday night.
If only I could straighten out
The tangled conundrum of my world

Which seems to happen best when I take the word straight to heart.

In The Palm Of God's Hand

Through fields of grass and water
Over meadows, streams, and floods,
I have come.

Reading texts, singing hymns, and reciting prayers
Walking down lonely streets under the glow of a light
Rest in the palm.

I've searched, sought, swept clean
And still fought battles
Until I really heard

God's hand.

The Choice You Make

Stairs leading to the second floor
The third and so forth to the top
Where you are greeted by Deity

The challenge starts.
Glass doors, errant kites, and backrubs
Walking, skipping, limping

Is it the past? Can't be the future.
Must be the present
Where you get a grip

Never ever saying never.

Church Testimony

In a church with Christian men,
I am waiting to give testimony
As I think back to the Fourth of July.

I remember the fireworks
That tried to outdo the sun and moon
As ruler of the sky.

The testimony I give would be great
If it could be so brilliant
and so exciting

That it would shine on in the minds of the men.

Container

The buds on the trees have bottled my attention
And the house behind them still holds the McCubrey's
Neighbors of my youth

Because after Mrs. McCubrey died
I saw her walking down the street.
When I looked again there was no one.

What could I do? There was no proof.
Only I know.
I believe angels come and go as they please,

But I'd like to bottle those buds on the trees.

A Smiley Parade

The 'Holi-Dazzle' parade carries its weight
In a spectacular light show
To carry us through the winter solstice.

You can't help but grin at the prospect of a parade in
December
Offering fairy tale characters bedecked in light bulbs
Dancing down the main street in town.

This night's special guests, The Rockettes,
Were placed on a float
While lesser dancers roamed freely.

It was all over after Santa Claus gloated on by.

Church Concert

The full body of the choir
With a sound like a carousel
Their mouths open like lakes.

Beethoven would have been proud
To see his Mass in C
Performed in such a stately study

On the Sunday morning.
Voices reaching for the Spire
Balanced as the three balconies

Inspirational as the sun through the stained glass windows.

On Stage With Dylan

In some kind of trance I looked
And I was on stage with Bob Dylan
Rocking my butt off

Singing all the songs that made him famous
Sharing smiles
Knowing that the audience was thrilled

I could hardly imagine that I was so cool
That we were sharing souls
That I could rock out

And for a while, I really liked myself.

Again Dylan

I had to go out and get a needle for my stereo
Because I hadn't listened to Dylan for a couple of weeks
Because my stereo had broken down from playing Dylan too much.

Dylan Thomas?, a poet would ask.
No Bob Dylan - a human would know
If not, you don't know me or anything about my life.

He stepped in when all else fell
He mesmerized my mind
He softened the blow to my heart

So again Dylan and again and again.

Running With Mick Jagger

I would start out in New York City
And cross the Atlantic in a fine ocean liner
Get over to Paris and have a bit of coffee.

I would go through Asia in a Rolls Royce
And in Japan I would visit a museum,
But in Australia I would talk music with an Aborigine.

I would come up through Africa in a jeep
And skip like a stone to South America
Careful to stop in Mexico and protest.

Then I would meet for a poetry reading at the Coffee Gallery.

Tap-Tap

Twiddle, twaddle for your supper
And sing in falsetto too.
No tap-taps in the U.S.

When I was in Haiti,
The cabs were called tap-taps,
And you tapped the driver to get out.

I suppose the requiem
At hand is faddle your fiddle
On your knees

If you knew the melody.

1000 Miles – Minneapolis 'n Dallas

An airplane ride carries
To Dallas Texas in February
Me, like first leaf of Spring.

Essentially, I'm there for business
But my pleasure is a woman friend,
And I combine them.

Plans, strategies, opinions, and views
Quiet conversation, hugs, and kisses
Goal forming and destination

1000 miles between them.

The Twin Cities

I walk out of the store
Close the door
Walk over to the corner.

A solitary figure
At the intersection
Of Franklin and Lyndale

But I'm not lonely.

Two million people of the Twin Cities stand there too.

How High I Go

I like to go downtown
To feel how high
The buildings go.

They show me
The nature of people
And what they will dare.

When I look up
I see peoples' dreams
Locked up block by block

In bold strategies that lean towards the sun.

Pick A Corner

The rabbit ran into the thicket
As I strolled to my spot on a curb
On the 4th of July.

I watched the fireworks through a frame
Of two taller buildings split by a shorter one
Making my view like a topless keyhole.

Am I lucky to be an American?
Undoubtedly. It certainly seems good
While from my safe distance

The night lights up in color.

Welcome

Nikes squishing the pavement
The dead reverberating on nearby hill
Ducks quacking in the opening of the ice

Cars streaming down streets
Nature unveiling its greens
The timely sun set in the sky

People talking, whistling, eyeing
Billions other places
Doing other things

Minneapolis, a humdrum on a Sunday.

Cool

Cool. I mean really cool
Where your wrongs
Only propel you to more coolness.

Think ice cream
Even hot water
But for now is cool.

Or how when it isn't,
Time will solidify
It all into a bundle

That is so cool it hurts.

Cold Night Wait

Not much happens when you're
Waiting for a bus
On a sub-zero Sunday night

Unless of course
You've just visited your mother
In a nursing home

Because she has advanced dementia
And because she still knows you
And things still matter.

Then a sub-zero night feels warm.

Frozen Thoughts

Sub-zero weather in hard on the mind.
All you try to do is to outlast the cold
And not let it into your head.

But it does get there
And a battle rages
But you're too cold to claim victory

Until you are home
And having paid the heating bill,
Your place is warm, and your thoughts thaw

And you build steam to do it again tomorrow.

Walking In Minnesota

I don't have far to go but it's so chilly,
Reminding me of the Arctic,
Somewhere I've only been in my imagination.

The clothes around me are a study in warmth:
Parka, boots, gloves, scarf and hat.
Just gives me the willies, so chilly.

That's the one thing they can't take away.
Minnesota will always freeze the body,
To the bone which is all right. I'll get by

If my soul greets it like a soldier.

Winter Played Its Trick

I had been taking the low road
Next to the lake where I was ready
To catch the sounds of spring.

I would have been sure of it
Seeing that all seemed lined up
For early arrival of that bursting season.

Just when I could have watched the ice crack,
We went into one of those late winter antics,
One of those 'we live in Minnesota'

One of those 'what were you thinking?'

Moments

It's In the Mail

The letter I said I'd send is in the mail.
So expect it soon as tomorrow or day after
Depending on fate or luck.

Then you will really know
What I really think
Because I didn't hold back

It's all there like a waterfall
Rushing over the edge
To a pool as deep as the earth

Down a river as long as time.

A Box

I only asked her to bring me the box.
She came back mad as hell
Saying, 'You're crazy. There's no box.'

I probably was crazy, but there was a box.
I saw it with my own two eyes.
It's something you don't need to prove.

You just know when you see one.
Did it vanish? I doubt it.
It must have been a coincidence,

A Prima Facie case of the elusive box.

Let's Do That Again

Recycle my dreams until they touch
The tricycles of yesterday
When wind howled amidst pelting rains.

Go back into my cave
Warmth of the fire
Summoning smiles like coins.

Tiptoe through gardens and over fences
Jungling past trash cans
Tipping over all that will.

Give me that good'ole sigh again.

Towel In, Towel Out

If I wear it then clean it too
Don't need a rubber stamp on that.
It's why the laundry basket has legs

Namely me. It will be nice when they
Invent a robot to do this.
I can't really wear things twice.

Grim and grime the marks of city life
A strangeness in my clothes,
My nakedness under control.

Isn't the heart clothed as well?

Can't Take It For Granted

A gift felt like it was given freely
Turned over to me like money
I say like money but more to it

Somehow I find it difficult to respond
But I feel I must do something
And not be a guru on a mountain top

Instead I'll cling to the course
But put one foot ahead of the other
Until I run out of road

Or lose my appetite for life.

Am I Salty Yet?

Once upon a time I lost my salt
And I felt my jewels of wisdom
Being trampled underfoot.

I'm not going to say what led up to this
Suffice it to say it was complex
And people were unable to help when they tried.

The hardest part was the hate
I felt from those who misunderstood me
And relegated me to their delete file.

Saw a lot of behinds then.

My Hands

My hands that follow a mind's nerves
Making their way along
Like a haybaler

Doing the work
Which was neglected
Or for other reasons set aside

And is now in the forefront.
The hands that could trouble
And bring ruin

Now stay busy with their own affair.

I Could Walk Through Walls

When the yellow ball of sun
Glows like laser flare on my mind
I could erase fear.

I could see myself grasping
The horse by the reins
Or shifting a car into fourth.

The fire of the sun
Burns between my ears
Like an automatic reaction

To the sensation of life.

Choice

It sounds so desirable, something
Somebody would covet
If they lacked options.

I've had my moments
Both when I did and when I didn't
Politics and love and health.

I hate to see someone stranded
At four-way stops
Or water going to its lowest level,

As compared to a butterfly in flight.

Don't Stop There

It's only a plateau of another mountain
Which is only half
The distance of a true stretch.

I usually play for the middle
But that's with economics
And class structure and that kind of thing.

When I'm on a journey I like to go the whole way
Spiveling especially towards the sun
Except when it gets too hot

And something must be done.

In Enemy Territory

Not especially feeling safe today
More like the fly on honey paper
A man who's lost his face.

But one who's found his direction
And taken a stance
Upon a rock.

The motion of an errant thrown stone
No longer a diversion
But a challenge

A talk with the perpetrator.

I See It Now

So, so sorry. I was blind.
You must admit a little guilt though.
Never should have thought we'd have a chance.

If ever there were star-crossed lovers.
We did share it for a second
And now for infinity.

But who made it possible?
Certainly our parents
Family, friends, and enemies.

Did we really even have enemies?

282

The Price Of Clarity

What's this buzzing, symphony or noise?
The cries come out of the earth
Next to disdain and discomfort.

If it wasn't a blue sky today
I'd be up a creek
Wondering what happened,

Or why I feel lost
Among so many.
I zip my jacket tighter.

Is it O.K. to scratch myself?

Ghosts Behind The Wheel

It's 5:30, dark, and snowing and I'm walking along
But I can't see who's driving the metal shells
That drift down the road

Like husks of corn on a conveyor belt.
The corncobs will find their way home
And strip themselves of the outer layers

Until they appear as kernels
Like the truths they tell each other
Safe from the maddening snow

And a world knee-deep in lies.

The Ongoing Traces

Essential yesterday's glories invoke roads
I would timidly avoid without the call
Received so many years ago.

Patented highways give the clue
On sunshine rays downed
To come to me like a father.

I hardly need the cereal of morning anymore
As I walk the path of my making
With steps that surround the earth

And knees that take their proper bow.

Like They Said

They always used to say,
'If you can't be good, be careful'
Back in the day.

And I try so hard to tiptoe
(Not always, but usually)
From my past to the present.

And I like thinking about the past now
Because I do have a present,
Despite all other attempts,

That came to me by being careful.

The High Road

What's the other choice? The low road?
You're given a choice. Make a decision.
Sometimes it's just up or down.

And it's not always a victory
Most often it's initially the harder
But there's payoff for going high.

The sky offers more freedom than the ground
And mountains have a really fine view.
An escape clause should be part of every contract

So take the stairs up and look around there.

Dreaming

I must be dreaming - pinch me.
There hasn't been a badly played song
On the radio all night.

The thermometer is even friendly
Full like a potato
But cool as ice tea.

Did you remember to bring the bags?
I'd be lost if I couldn't transport
My things.

I must be lost but found.

Those Bad Choices

I've made some real wrenchers in my time
Because of weakness or poor planning
Left me in a fit of discomfort.

But I've always had the humility
To go down on my knees
Before the Almighty

Who wrestles away my guilt
Like an omnipotent psychiatrist
Leaving me whole

Able to walk down the path another day.

The Meds

I swallow the pills like castor oil
Which will purge my mind
And cleanse the system

As I ask myself,
'What of me?'
'Am I a test case?'

I pinch my leg.
It's still there
I am more than a white rat.

More like a vacuumed attic.

Stability

You'd never know if you just listened
All of the arguing.
Some movies are pure chaos too.

But hand me a book of Statutes
And you'll see
There's only two sides

But the power is being drained
By the mighty
Leaving bones

Can't we plug the dyke?

Take The Picture Already

From my safe perch in my windowless office,
Winter has called me into his Minnesota omnipresence
Suggesting that I had some important matter.

No, not really. Although, I could be a little excited.
It will be on the front page
And I'm almost playing hooky.

My breath is a legacy
And my footprints an autograph.
I almost need sunglasses.

Hurry up will you? The cold is melting me.

It All Comes Back To This

History rules, time offers
Money and gardens
Winnowing attention from the headlines

Been treated like a migrant infant
At times, far away in front
Too cool to touch

In my chair for the duration
Opening and closing all accounts
Drifting…

Saved by the ringing phone.

Embracing The Challenge

You don't have to live too long
Before you must make choices –
You only get so much freedom.

Even if you follow a path
It often splits into two or more
Avenues leading to quite different places.

Many times the difference is clear
Even though not easy but hard
And there is usually a price to pay,

Either at the start or the end of the road.

What A Joy

I just want to soak the moment in
It won't be forever, but then again
I will always remember it

Just like the many times you helped me out
When voices ravaged my mind
And you calmed the turbulence.

Now we're having dinner over memories
Both good and bad but always honest
As I try to pry loose once again

To go out and accomplish what you've already done.

I'll Tread Lightly

I'm in new area so I'll go slowly
Like the water in a winding stream
Always onto the new.

I'll just go in until it's at my ankles
The sand holding up my feet
My body my anchor.

I want to look around
New to the neighborhood
I want to be safe

Under an umbrella, my shelter.

Streetlight Night

The streetlight
Spots
The roadway.

I got my start
One night
Under a streetlight.

The brightness
Piercing
My inner darker mind.

I've never regretted streetlights at night.

I Listen To Myself

Sometimes when nobody else will listen
I listen to myself
Like the sound of a well

And I take great solace
When I think that others
Can still enter my life

At my deepest point of need.
And you're one of those
Who I count on

An old oak on a country hillside.

Cover To Cover

It opens like a budding leaf
Singular and delicate
Tasteful and innocent.

It moves like a river
Edging away the channels of my mind
And laying my thoughts down a wide current.

The words portray a heartbeat
And sing their life
Into my soul

A butter knife spreading goodness.

Experience

A pine tree out of my second story window
An open prairie from state beyond state
Or a crusty football coach calling signals.

I glimpse, then look, and I gawk
Seeming to go deeper into the well
Springing up into a firmer grasp.

Seismic realities next to gentle fawns
Displays of grandeur with knowledge
Some smiles but more nods

Bastion of a lake.

Mid-April Snow

Out of my apartment and into the elements
The snow and wind into my face
As I take an afternoon jog.

Snowflakes line the rim of my cap,
And the wind howls around my striding body
On this mid-April mid-day run.

We could be looking ahead to winter
Not behind.
Because it's springtime now

The snowfall is just an unusual escape.

Warming Up

The rain is gently falling on my umbrella
As I notice the first few strands of green grass.
Today's twigs will be tomorrow's branches.

That's why I refuse to ride the bus
Instead I choose to walk
Through the awakening park

Which makes me feel a bit elated.
The whole city is in tune with a spring dance
Where life begins over for me

Waiting to see that first robin before I believe.

Then Summer

Take off that jacket, summer's here.
After a no-show on spring
I was awakened by summer.

Trees unholding their leaves
That must have appeared at night
Because weather was offish.

Sun shining just like I remembered it
Now thinking of new freedoms
Following from outdoor skies

That open my heart to warmth.

The Things I Live For

Something that is brittle in the fall,
That hardens in winter, blossoms in spring,
And eats in summer,

Is my life
As I'm drifting down
A nameless street in St. Paul.

It's the change of seasons I think
The new way to look at things
And scope it all out

As I develop a method to watch.

Night Walk Home Fall

Why as the leaves fall
Do I clutch my heart harder?
Is it resistance, something the leaves don't have?

Couldn't I be shrewder
Knowing I've passed this way
Before and winter won't bite.

Or will it? My face an icicle
Pointing to a cold heart...
No! I will not abandon the ship

Instead, set my gaze and romp.

Winter Flower

Wisp light bouquet, a shiver of happiness
Brought together in the form
Of a flower.

Still skyward bending
Bloom of the season
A bit too good to pass by.

I must have inherited the wealth
Coming at me as a surprise
On these warm days in December.

Though I could have known better.

294

Winter Shroud

Cold crystals coming from the sky
Who knows how
But it's clear something's happening.

A hospital gown over the dead earth
And us trying to stay alive
If we can just get to that building

But the snow blinds me
Yet I can still trace the outline
Of someplace warm

Not much gets done on nights like this.

Floor

I've been working on floors
After I took that fall
From the sky.

I've been shining them
While I was there
And since I had the time.

I know what it means
To be on
The bottom -

To touch cold ground.

The Shaft

Centrally situated, pulleys, chains hidden
I board with trust of my life
In the mechanics of the building.

Door knob to the top floor,
Compartmentalized feelings.
I'm glad I don't have phobias.

It's been a smooth ride
I offer to the imaginary attendant.
There's even the bell.

Consider myself one up.

The World I Can't Contain

I learned all right if you don't take the stairs
You won't go anywhere,
And escalators are no work at all.

Gravity's pull is daunting,
Yet, yearning for the light of heaven is stronger.
Who digs holes without special needs?

Any pleading we hear is only for hope,
A sizing of the scope it takes
In order to spring as a sprinter

And forget constrictions that bind like skins.

Why I Broke The Lamp

I was the square hole, a subject to the many
Round pegs being thrust my direction
Similar to cigarettes at a confirmation ceremony.

But it was a last straw when they
Locked the door and took the key,
And the door had to be yellow.

My last defense in my repertoire
My answer to the charges before me
A shocker meant to express

The unequal condition presented to me.

Flight

Jet lag stifling me on the ground
When yesterday I looked out over clouds
And there was just enough of a wing I could see.

Assurance that I am through and eventually
Does ease foreseeable horizons.
The flight was even if not fairly gained.

Now I wander kicking imaginary rocks,
Combing hair, washing laundry -
Doing the things that are needed.

I may never fly again, but I'll hold my ticket just the same.

Airport Traffic

Watching movement in the airport hub
Reminds me of a schoolyard playground
With pockets of people in various poses.

Some take to the sportsbar and the TV
Others seem in never-ending motion
While still others idle in their seats.

I want to take them all up
and file them down into their plane
Where they'll be safely on their way,

Which of course is exactly the way it is.

Computer Graced

Let me go into the land of no return
Where I can entertain kings
Or see space come to life.

Why worry when everything is
The touch of a button
Like a partner in creating

Webs of imagination
Giving me knowledge like a book.
Only my mind

Can nix the flow with a switch.

Ton Of You

Heap it on go ahead go for it
It's like what I've been waiting for
What signal are you seeing? - the light is green

Dress to the nines, put down the roof, open your eyes
Don't stop there at which you are
Go blank, tighten your laces

I am catching a drift of you
But my feet are numb
Suppose anything you want...

Catch that wave, scale the wall, dive in

Day

Links of sunshine, early, really early,
And shoe steps of me toppling
Stairs, sidewalks, and stairs.

I am a middleperson in messages
A lick here a stamp there
And off you go.

Surprised by the end to go home
Stairs, sidewalks, stairs
Is that all I do?

I think I'll stop for a pop.

Iceberg

Snow pounds down on my blue cap
And over the sidewalk as if the heavens
Were a mint and the clouds were banks.

My heavy steps don't even touch cement
Though the snow is packed as hard.
It is a creation of lopsided treachery.

Who would think that such puffery
Would wield snarls of slipper
Upon the unbelieving souls beneath

Who flee to homes where they thaw.

On

Taut like a tennis net.
No shots out of bounds
On this court.

The fur has worn off the ball;
The racket lean as a nail.
A fence surrounds play

If you could call it that.
I wonder whether it's still a game,
Or maybe it's a match

That will ignite all.

Can Still Go On

Thank God I haven't told all my secrets
Just enough to crest at sea
With the other gapers and tourists

In this town/city
Where Economics is a mantle
Placed on the shoulders of the unknown

And justice is struggled against
Each other
Like teardrop passion plays

And if you're lucky you still have some at day's end.

Torchlighter

Shifts of participants steady
And we, the rest, rest before
The sun goes down.

We are rails of a track
Octopi displaced
The coming of a train

And we are not disappointed
Night flow of entertainment
Different marchers

In the ongoing...

Stepping Easy

Easy does it down the street
Walking over trodden ways.
I'm hopeful to miss the holes

Which could delay me
Or send me into a tizzy –
Flight from the knowing to unknown.

I just walk easy,
Don't get in the way
As I juggle my body

And lightly press on.

Guiding Windows

The bus patrons and their destinations
Which pound out sense
In our tour of the city.

Twigs barking from the trees of their
Unyielding foundations
Tiny spirits whose bareness says winter.

And the driver with duties
While we survey
Keeping close in our hearts

Glad to be traveling and grasping how far we've come.

Holidays Can Soothe

Take a holiday and mix it with
One part – easy chair
Two parts – magazines

And what you have is
A nice blend of relaxation
That tempers all those work days

And offers up a warm inhalation
On an otherwise hurry-blurry day.
Not that I wish I was on permanent holiday

But their interspersed gifts are welcomed.

Salvation Army Bell Ringer

Beacon in the winter, you totem pole of Christmas,
You are like a peppermint in cellophane,
Or is that celluloid, a star.

Your music rolls down from rhythmic strokes of the wrist
Each chime an expectation of joy,
Or is it a smile in fruition.

You're out here standing when all else moves
And you give us pause to drop a little in your pail,
Or do we take your glance

As our moment of the season's offering.

In My Dreams

In my last dreams shortly before I awake
I'm sure I'm thinking about my apple
That I will have to start my day.

In the shower as I lather up
Juices in my mouth
Begin to come alive.

As I pack my apple into my satchel
I am imagining
All the health held in that piece of fruit

A virtual keg of power.

I Found The Cross

An angel grabbed my heart
And led me on a long path
To the cross.

I wasn't always clear where I was headed
But it seemed like the only place to go
As troubling and disconcerting as it was.

The payoff made me speechless
And it was years until I found my feet again.
Don't know why I missed it so many years

And why suddenly it was there.

Thanks

Thanks for the moment at the cross
It was hard to bear
But someone made it less so

A voice over the radio
Some anonymous kind soul
With a sigh that struck deep

Then I was able to gather myself
Listen to a little music
A shift of direction

And it didn't hurt that you rose from the grave.

What Falls From Skies

When I began to gain a knowledge
Of the expanse of the universe
I categorized it with science.

Oh sure, I used the moon romantically,
And the sun as a simile.
At times I thought I was a star.

But can you see? Can you imagine?
How unprepared I had grown
To anything happening

Like the angel dropping into my heart.

I'll Follow My Angel

Many, many could be distractions
But I don't let it stop me.
Preciously time lingers

In front of my eyes like sand.
It's mostly excitement
In something I can't prove.

But that will get them,
Even if I wanted it to.
No, it's not what I get.

It's the freedom I witness.

Sin

In the sacred walls within my church
Within my heart
I'm able to watch my sin fly.

A holy setting, an ideal place
For me
To let them go.

I can raise my eyes
To the stainglass windows
And see

Like a sheep his home in the hay.

Where Were You?

What escape route did you take
To evade that question?
When did you fall into the night?

I drank of that light until
The sun was a toy
And the moon was becoming powerful.

Then like you I rested
In more serene fields
Caught my breath

Made my atonements.

A Word

Everyone has a word that chills his soul
Reeling away from the light
Dispersing the strong like straw.

If you question this,
Consider what blasphemy
Does to God.

You can build legions
To protect your heart
But, 'puff' and you're gone.

Only well-trained professionals can...

The Escalator

When you've made your decision
To step on
You're either going up or down.

You may be going up
Like Christ to the mountaintop to be transfigured
Only you're going up to Wards to try on clothes.

You may be going down
Like Moses carrying the Ten Commandments
Only you're carrying fries and a hamburger.

Up or down the escalator will take you there.

Symphony Concert

The sweet music flows from
Structured hands
To an appreciative audience.

Sounds somewhere between
Melancholy and sunshine
Hover over dark suited musicians.

I listen with great concentration
Paying my respects
To the civilized manners

That lift me to dignity.

Clean

Whether I am holding a broom
Or lifting my soul up to God
I am cleaning.

I may be fumbling for a dustball
Or regretting a misdeed
However, I am doing the same thing.

It's not about sweeping up dirt!
The idea is to make a building cleaner
Or a soul more pure

Like the stream I drank from in the Colorado Rockies.

The Nature Look (2)

The bend of the willow tree is very erotic
Especially in the wind as today
I am only a substitute

Or, skipping over the ice on skates
A boy with dreams.
Opposed to grasping,

Where you can hear the song
Birds calling me?
But from my window

I am a foreigner anxious over deportation.

Missing You

The song of your life may still be in the air
And talk of you may still surround me
But you've been unhinged

And blown away like autumn leaves.
Even though you're there; you're not.
I miss our phone calls, our conversations

And the otherworldliness of our relationship
Has changed the game.
I have more room now

And less space.

Her Contribution

She is reckless like a garter snake
Singing songs to the open air
Wringing water out of her hair.

I focus on what she has given to me
In the form of new life
And stairsteps to her room.

The picture presents erect postures
With glad smiles for all
And a clarity for the moment

Coupled with a warm bosom.

Middle Of The Night

It is the middle of the night
And you're probably in bed
So I won't call.

Anything I have to say
Can wait until the morning
Or into the afternoon.

You're sleeping soundly now
And I don't want to disturb you
From your sleep

And I probably don't have anything to say.

Just A Wink

I was only slipping you a nod,
A wink, saying, 'Hi'.
Wasn't intentionally disrespectful.

Something about you attracted me
And needed response
Salute.

The world turns the same way
Sun will rise and set
A watch will still spin twice

Just a wink.

Standing There

I saw you and I knew you knew
Because of a smile
And that look.

You know the look
It's the one that
Could start a forest.

Anyway, you knew that I knew
It didn't matter
That we were on a city street,

Everyone knew.

Returning To The Bridge

Almost forgotten the day
Driving; I mean riding,
Across a bridge with a friend.

Bright sunny, a warmth
Just when
She was walking along

With her friend.
My friend and I
Looked at her friend and her

And we all smiled.

312

The Corner Garden

Yellow tulips balance on their stems
Crystal goblets full of wine
Honey for the bumbling bees.

The trucker comes down the road
Eclipse of my imagination
Wake up call to my seated self

He will be home tonight
Flowers in his sheets
Two lips pressing

To create nectar in lovers' veins.

Big Trucks

A big truck rolled down the road
As I walked down the street -
Humpf, humpf. Wow-bow, wow-bow.

The driver gassed the engine
Aroom, aroom.
Humpf, humpf. Wow-bow, wow-bow.

He was something like 16 feet off the ground
And he chewed a cigar
Looking at me from the corner of his eye.

Aroom, humpf. Wow-bow, wow-bow.

More Work

Not long after the overnight packages are done
I'm getting ready to process the certifieds
Which, like the overnights, are entered on the computer.

My head is clear and the work is a breeze.
I'm feeling healthy like a good economy
And I cruise through the certifieds

Like I'm knocking down dominoes.
Then there's a lull
Where I catch up on things

Or just relax for a few moments.

The Tall Man

The tall thin man shuffles hamburgers
At the burger emporium
On successive days – Monday though Friday.

He doesn't matter the nameless customers
Because he's so concerned
About not burning the burgers

Steady Eddy - the man flipping 'em
Working and thinking
Wondering.

Not overly happy - it's just a job.

The Tightrope

High above the artist walks
The thin path over the rope
Miles above the crowd.

Impressive the view,
But dangerous the height,
Still clasping a bar for balance.

Just the purpose
Is as far from his mind
As cats and water

Because he finds himself lost.

Unbound

No seams or zippers
They've all been cast off
Like rain oil a windshield.

Pictures gone
Memories torn
Bare trees in the winter

Free to go
Shackles unclasped
Glass spilled

Dawn

A Hint Of Happiness

This morning, on the way to work,
Amidst the tired
Travelers,

With openness,
Freely,
And very gaily,

A woman passenger
Told the busdriver
Some joke... some anecdote,

And my face warmed with a smile.

Forget About 13 Blackbirds

Thousands where I am by the bus.
This park levies fear in its trees
Where I wonder if I'll be attacked.

Hitchcock's not around
So I wonder what's up with these birds
In this nocturnal gathering.

I've been to baseball games, seen crowds…
But there's no food here…is there?
Still they sit

Eerie like being stalked or something.

Brace Against The Wind

You stood, a tree forming
Sending roots, branches, bark
Like a residence of Earth

You basement in a storm
An ice over water
Glue onto the paper airplane I was

Caught a leaf
Not resting
Until

The kite was rolled home.

'I'll Take That Bus'

Drifts of snow between the forgotten spring
And my soul heartened knowing it can't go on
As a winter intruding on my warmth.

A vehicle is able to maneuver the ice
Roughly cracking the cold block by block
In my bus as it tours winter wonderland.

Me? I'm safe I guess behind the glass window
Perched in my observatory
Packing, packing, packing

A snowball that is never thrown.

Running After It

I'm running after it.
And I have been for some time now
Starting with jogging shoes and shorts.

I go maybe a couple of miles,
Or on some days a whole bunch.
It's running with desire

There's something I'm chasing
That I know I'll find
Because I had it before,

And I'll get it by running.

City People And Homes

The houses all look
So unique
Like individuals living there

As I imagine them
As the bus passes by.
The people with me on the bus,

Are city people.
They seem diverse – a dichotomy.
The two ways to see people

Means I must look through two eyes.

Sizing Up Downtown

Stubborn buildings grip at the
Molten sidewalks
Passageways of the fleeing

Whose escapage was once
The other way of flight, to,
Not from, this central hub.

What seasoned meat is rejected
For its flavor? The outer rings are a
Dandelion puffed by wind.

Why is that crane knocking down that building?

What's In Those Buildings

These buildings with their advertised awnings
And horizontal neon invitations
Which make me want to go inside.

They're across the street from my busstop
I'll be late if I take the time to go over
So it'll have to wait.

I sure bet there's surprises there though
Which I could never glean
From where I'm standing.

They've built me out for now.

It's Sunday

It's Sunday and I'm resting
Like a book on the shelf
Or a picture on the wall.

Millions of things I could be doing
Thousands of ways to spend time
Hundreds of places to go

But I'm at home in my condo
Writing this poem
Comfortable like a down jacket

There's tomorrow, but for now…

Going Now

Beyond the stick, past the ball,
Through the book, above the lamp
Over the PC, on top of the window.

With my feet I will walk.
Transformations sifting reality
Thunderstruck.

I'm alone always alone
Conquering, conquesting yesterdays
Until the uprising

Is little more than a haughty glance.

Love Is All About Easy

The best way to get a handle is by being loose
And the most interesting path to a point
Is a zigzag with short pauses.

I've discovered more through serendipity
Staying open past the night
Trolling like a fishing boat

Watching the smiles come
Blurring tangents into circles
Orbs of light reflecting

Until the prisoners release, song of the sparrow.

I'm On The Tip Of The Leaf

The butterfly arises from the street - tar and stones,
And takes flight into the sunlit afternoon.
In a sometimes erratic fashion

It flies past me towards the bridge by Cedar Avenue
Where by a building it finds a tree.
Walking closer, closer so I can get a better look

I find the butterfly
About head high.
And in my mind's eye I am with her

On the tip of the leaf, at the stretch of the stem.

When I Think About It

If I am able I like to remember where I have been
In former lives on some other planet
In someone else's clothes spending someone else's money.

But I have a hard time with this and it is probably best
Because my life was not all it was cracked up to be
And was far less than I imagined it was.

They were quite clear that I was delusional;
Things that occurred to me didn't occur to anyone else
Try as hard as I might to have it otherwise

And it still only holds meaning when I think about it.

The Old Records

Music of my former lives spins
Me lying teary-eyed
Not missing one intonation.

Where did it all go?
Which meant so much?
How could it? How did it?

I could ransack those albums for a lifetime
And still wonder.
Isn't it ironic that I never thought I'd be old

And say those were the days.

The Complexity

Prisms inside out lofted then ditched
To hold the cause for a micro-second
While the wall stands unblemished.

Not even a wink thinking
Vast and minute sums
Never mind the ceiling.

Before then better than computers
Almost paralysis
I could hardly stay in my chair.

We were on earth that evening.

Great Arios – 46 poems

Personal

Creak

The thin line between your heart and mind
Is narrow like a choice
But written verse which swings.

Your mostly impregnable fortress repels most attempts
As if there were all the gold of the Pharoahs
At stake in your smile.

Won't you let me sing you a song?
I yearn to speak sweet everythings in your ear,
Take you for a trip into your dreams,

Allow me the creak of your heart.

Like A Child

She was a child disarmingly cute, sassy
Seemingly had never known loss
Or wore it on her dress.

Hard won toughness a knife in my heart.
On to the next thing always building
Never revealing behind those brown eyes.

But then she was a child in the way she left me
Not peacefully but grabbing for the money
So much better than me she thought.

To the arms of someone who also thought he was better.

Square World

Everything about America is so linear
Straight to the heart an arrow
slicing the cake into halves.

Even the doctors give shots
Through the skin paths
measured in centimeters.

Can you bum me a square?
He asked,
Not even knowing my name.

I made a big mistake when I gave away my grandmother's rocker.

Good Grief

A famous singer who I respected said,
'Good work is never done until the mourning comes'
And I believe it was 'mourning' not 'morning.'

I went through my boyhood never feeling grief
It was all laughter and on to the next laugh
Until my Grannie died and returned to me as an angel.

Grief, grieving, grove, grieven, grievous
Good, better, cleansing, reflection, solitude
Water, tears, sleep, music, maturity, God

Never ceasing, carry me to the next day.

Road Signs

A long walk and you'll see
Plenty of signs that grab your attention
For a minute, sometimes a year or more.

If you don't have a camera
Get out your notebook
Or your billfold and buy it.

The best signs are from above
But buried ones are more fun
Floating ones can take you along

'No sign of him.' You can bet that's a lie.

How Could They Know?

It was done in private with no one else home
When the world was going on without me
Except for the setting sun and rising moon.

I didn't think you'd hear or see me
Or ever know or wonder why
It was just between me and me.

So now I know you don't know
Because you weren't there
You can only guess

Time has a way of protecting me.

The Dog In Heaven

Confronting the contradictions in the Bible
Was quite a proposition
For me - a wannabe Christian,

I didn't like to see
Anything left out of something
So beautiful.

I'm referring to Revelations.
I was okay with leaving out
Murderers, idolaters, even the sexually immoral,

But somehow I just couldn't agree with leaving out the dogs.

Running Through The Names

I've gotten to the point where I'm running through the names:
Abraham Lincoln, Christ, Mohammed, and Buddha, Anne Sexton.
Honest, spiritual, and poetic.

In time's eye they all seem to be One of an orchestra,
Part of a plan: Mark Twain, Hermann Hesse, Thomas Edison,
    Vincent Van Gogh.
They ease my situation: Margaret Mead, Betty Ford, Bob Dylan.

If only that dropping names was cool.
Harmon Killebrew, Mark Spitz, names that I've heard
Some tied to faces, places, and

Frames of reference for my Bruce Ario.

Minneapolis

Out To The Store

I stepped out to the store
To get the vitamins
That the doctor wants me to take.

The glass danced in the windows of the shops,
Closed now at this later hour,
And cars flowed down the busy avenue.

On my way home from the store
I noticed the iciness of the sidewalk
And a small group of teenagers

Separating my business from theirs and the rest of the city.

Indications

The highway crew spins yarn from their coffee as I
Pass down the vein back into Minneapolis.
Road construction riveted into my being like sound.

There will be a better road to travel - to get to know
Eventually. As it grows perpendicular to this city
There is a hint of growth suppressed only by material limits.

I'm really ageless the changes going on around me
Don't stop or settle because that's all there is.
And I don't mind really even though I can't keep up

I try with one more line... one more eyeful... another taste of it.

The Parameters Of Downtown Minneapolis

The breadth of downtown Minneapolis
Can be seen in the breadth of countless red taillights
Leaving on one way streets going out

To suburbs and other hidden places
While downtown lingers in my mind
And upon my feet that know I'm not leaving.

The height of downtown Minneapolis
Is witnessed in buildings
Etching their designs upon my opened face.

And the depth is seen by perceiving eyes.

My Coffee And I

At five o'clock I'm off work,
And by five-thirty
I meet my cup of coffee downtown.

I'm on the skyway sipping
From my cup -
So warm and good.

The people I watch below from above
Look like they're part way -
More than nothing, but less than full.

My cup and I finish with a heavy gulp.

Another Night Coming Home

Out of the deli
After a meeting
To a busstop.

It's ten o'clock
Been going since six this morning
I'm yawning under a streetlight.

The cars scurry down the road
Storekeepers leave their stores
Police walk the beat.

The busstop grows crowded.

Philosophy

Sequence

The green leaves hover just over the trunks,
And women's tennis shoes plod the downtown sidewalks.
I get a bite out of myself in a glass window at a bank.

We emerge from the left lane and go 55 on the Express.
If only I could taste the toe of realism;
I am left to houses split in two by the interstate.

At home there's a plate of food; a book too.
I'll eat the humble meal that I bargained for
And go places I've already been

From places I could only believe in.

In Someone's Garden

Once, I attempted to be a flower,
Straightest distance to the sun
For the warmth I felt when a woman

Placed one in the GI's barrel.
The garden is borrowed, for no one
Can stop flowers this season

Coronation of beauty with
Delicacy of an eyelash.
What makes them grow?

Only half of it's arbitrary.

Park Trees

...Or your city trees with their leaveness
Would oblige me one step further
On this evening walk.

Transparent you, you photosynthesizers
I will linger on your moon
Follow strewn asphalt.

Perhaps you see me
Ducking under your plume
Seizing the greenness

Until the matter you are.

Living The Snowfall

The snow drifts like a sonnet from the sky
In small flakes of neon.
It lights up the coldness and makes me smile.

In pockets on the ground blown together
It makes a blanket across the city
Covering the barren gray ground.

I wonder where it all came from -
(I mean besides the clouds).
A sparkling form

Too real to disregard or misunderstand.

Just As It Was

The moon isn't quite the way it was
Last month it was over there
And it seemed lighter in the sky.

But I'm on the same bus bench
As I have been for some time now
Whether tonight or the last 30 years.

Change seems so difficult
Genuine change
Anybody can change clothes

But few can move the moon from there to there.

My Second Favorite Celestial Ball

Waking to that positive in the air
Some 92 million miles away
My destination, here

A grown sponge of a man
Soaking for all it will give.
Doesn't matter, doesn't count its

Centeredness. I'm a daffodil
Of freckles speculating for my marbles
Which happen to glow right now,

Which could never cover my relief and stay still light.

The World I Can't Contain

I learned all right if you don't take the stairs
You won't go anywhere,
And escalators are no work at all.

Gravity's pull is daunting,
Yet, yearning for the light of heaven is stronger.
Who digs holes without special needs?

Any pleading we hear is only for hope,
A sizing of the scope it takes
In order to spring as a sprinter

And forget constrictions that bind like shells.

The Wall's Gone

My legs are two cartons of milk,
And the lake where I lumber
Has drifted toward spring.

The grass is perplexed between
Green and yellow
Nomads loosen their grip

Me a song
The longer I run the less far I get
It's all one big ball now

The quest for freedom found

Suppose I...

Before I run my pen down,
Sitting here makes me wonder.
If I dreamed of you longer

Would I total a different view
Of things about you
That would arrive some new

Summation. What divi-
dend spiraling down from heaven
Could come to this end?

...circular game that it is.

Something To Say

I always thought I had something to say
Even when others said it for me.
Better to have words put in your mouth

Than a dagger in your heart.
But when I was given a pen
I went straight to work

Like a truck driving down the road
Or a swallow singing a morning song
No word too unimportant to say

Or as important as the next one.

I've Been A Word

I've been a word in a poem
A song in the air
And a note of music.

The thinness of my soul at times
Has caused me to look
Enviously at handrails or trees

Don't bump me
While I dissolve;
Give me more time...

Another way to last.

The Fullness Of Time

Tempered by the hand of God
Time exists like space
Or something equally senseless.

Gripping me as would a vice
I am surrounded by
Its thump, thump, thump.

Prettier than music
I like time
For its gaiety of being

Reminding me of an inexpensive watch.

Apparent Scope

My life sashayed into a train
Running far faster than legal limits.
I was thrown out of the passenger seat like a pit.

There I met dogs, thieves and victims
Occasionally with light in their lives -
A place to rendezvous and start up

For a match I could only sense.
I couldn't hardly rise to take my seat
Among the others who didn't know

Where I was or where I was going to.

Pickings

Sensitively rendered ones are good.
And unexpected ones as well.
I especially like bright, shiny ones.

Oftentimes I must stoop to get them.
Or grasp them out of the air.
But that's hard if it's windy.

Some graciously appear of their own right.
While others are dug out.
Pulled, stretched, or excavated.

It's the getting I'm after.

Moments

Marching

I'm chasing the song in the wind
Light from the sun my goal.
Sidewalks crumble under my feet

Through buildings, concrete, air
But with a subtle discrimination
Towards the hopeful, the reasonable.

Holding back nothing; holding back everything.
Offending no laws; stretching no boundaries
A walk into the future like a river.

Sleeping under the illumed moon.

Only Angels Above Me

The Starlings rattle in the grass,
Cars meander home from work,
And I ambulate down the street.

Perhaps it's almost too easy:
The conveniences of America
As I drink the air and survey.

The real villainry pushed aside like a garbage bag
In which I fought my battle of self,
In which rosebushes were cut down

And tossed upward until they escaped gravity.

The Crawl

Not my choice to be down on the ground,
Can't even sidestep the puddles
Which appear oversized and long.

Once I could skip over it all
Like a bike ride down gravel
Until my fenders came loose

And it ended as though a period.
I'm a night crawler, and would be a pagan
If there wasn't a little light left

Up towards that hill and over that way.

Stretched In A Tree

The tree trunk -
Thick, rough, and cumbersome
To look at.

The branches and twigs
Present something more interesting
in their non-parallel way.

I am lost in the tangle
As if the branches intended to trap my gaze
That they're meant not only to hold the bird's nest but me.

I escape, though, by watching the upward reach of all there is.

Infinity

Where does the bath water go when
It downs the drain into the river
And to the ocean?

Could I bathe myself in its immensity
by sounds that tat-a-tat
On my window?

If the sky walked into my life,
Or the ocean, would you know
Someone you don't already?

As if that hasn't already happened.

Searching For A Laugh

Searching for a laugh is a serious business
In today's world where nothing is off the cuff
And throats are tighter than a straw.

You've got to know where to not look
Funny is absence, out of body
Our natural state is funny

Which should rule
Which doesn't for sin and greed prevail
But it's funny when the wicked are in our sights

Then timing, timing, timing.

I'll Whisper It

Can you handle it if I just whisper it?
I won't come in with the guns blazing
Just warm intentions, smiling.

Have a rendezvous but in the light
Under the shadow of a tree
Out in the midst of the woods

Just as day breaks we will embrace
As though we can't get enough
Of each other's unspent attention.

Then, then... then.

The Way You Did It

That night on the boat might have been weird
But it wasn't.
Love yes, but nothing sexual or stimulating.

It was two men and a transfer of power.
Me the underling trying to rise
And you in control and coming down to me.

Nobody else saw it; no witnesses.
Yet if I told that story to someone
The truth would be evident

Enough to warrant a second thought, and a third…

Three Days In New York

The first end of it
Is the boardroom eyes
Perusing narrow sheets of typed paper.

Then time it takes us
Out to a comedy show
Riding in cabs fastly in the dark.

The touchdown, pinnacle, coup de grace
Is dinner with her in Greenwich Village.
We part with a kiss and a wave.

Three days past now but firm in memory.

Where Has It Gone?

Burning up the calendar
Like a gas guzzling SUV
I look over my shoulder

Realizing no ultimate politeness
Will bring back the summer
And I could have never saved

Even a blade of grass
To blow a whistle
Stop the game

No, NO. It's time to gather poles.

Train Coming

Tracked. Don't give'em everything they ask,
Just what they worked for.
Land passes by

And out the windows
Life is what it seems
Or much more than possible.

Suppose I settle in
Suppose I give up support
Suppose I just ride

I really hope the headlights are shining.

Speculation On Dots

Highly blended dabs as a surface
Rebound the mirror of minds
Come to on waves from somewhere else.

Eager to differentiate the glows
Opposing preconceived opinions
Wax now in sleep.

To the contrary, amusement plays keys
On a piano of dreams in the sky
Bluer than your cold lips

Or a lexicon from your general direction.

Why'd You Do That?

Grace walked down the sidewalk and swallowed
My heart like a Nabisco cracker. It wasn't until
Years later I was able to look up at what happened.

My time had come. The day was done.
Either get it or get out.
Why don't you grow up?

But it put trouble on the run
And bounce in my step to think
Everything was at stake

And nothing was lost… like a sunset.

Not Every One Is… If Only They All Were.

Birds would find it difficult to go through a square birdhouse hole
In the same way cars would be standstilled with triangular tires.
Pluto with a rectangled orbit would look strange.

Why is it then, squares seem to take such a prominent place?
Homes are really circular when you think of
The paths you make to from and around.

Wouldn't you fall off the edge if life were flat?
Why can't we see that clocks are round?
Who's been laying that straight highway?

I've been reading about Haiti… now there's a square peg.

Quarters, Nickels, And The Rundown

The change in my pockets clinks
In the bottom
Like a part of an automobile not working.

Legs taut and tight
My sneakers making the pace
I run towards the lake.

I reach the water
To hear geese greeting spring
Just as they fly overhead

And my change in my pocket is silent.

Take Your Stance

Mis-aligned autos tour roads
Past shiny rows legalized as apartments
Where I am a dot on a busstop.

Atoms collecting in interesting patterns
It seems to me anyway, because I am one
Which my forebears made sure of.

Funny you should ask about trees.
I don't know where the roots
Dig in, anymore than anyone else.

Anyhow you look at it, it's tin vs. bark.

Daily

Melting down a sandwich at a fastfood,
Evening out a bus ride with the poor,
I cruise through green lights like a jet.

It's a course, a river, a labyrinth
That I must pass through to glory.
That waits like a flag perched on a pole.

But it's much more. More like a flower,
Whose stem supports the blossom.
When I thought I would bend down,

I find I must stand up.

What Is This Wind?

The marionetted leaves filter
Power lightly taking
The images before me.

Invincible courier of my imagination
Defeat of gravity. All else
Locking my mind.

Blow through me until
I am transported
Into that special place

To stand against your whimsy.

I'll Sign Off For Now

Now much going on upstairs
So I decided to pick up
A new language.

A co-worker
Is Hearing impaired
Unable to communicate to me.

Taking the two conditions
Becoming aware
I decided to learn

_____!

Made in the USA
Columbia, SC
15 November 2024

46510306R00189